CONSPIRACY OF THE IN

Patrick Regan is an unsung hero. His organisation, XLP, does extraordinary work among young people in tough places. It is no wonder that they won the inaugural Queen's Golden Jubilee Award for voluntary service by groups in the community. Patrick's encouraging story will inspire many others to work within inner city areas and see them transformed through God's love.

Nicky Gumbel
Holy Trinity Brompton

Patrick Regan is the real deal. His heart of compassion, humility and service among the poor and marginalised has been a constant source of challenge and encouragement to me. Full of amazing stories, this book will inspire you to live differently and make a difference.

Tim Hughes
Director of Worship, Holy Trinity Brompton

Patrick Regan and XLP have been on the front lines for years, meeting the 'last and least of these' throughout South London with a message of great worth and vision for a different kind of life. I've seen their work up close and know both the struggle and the exuberance that simultaneously ooze from their inner-city outreach in the toughest parts of town. In *Conspiracy of the Insignificant* their story is powerfully and practically portrayed, a model for what can happen in cities around the globe and a must-read for anyone seeking to breathe the hope of Jesus into the generation to come. A compelling glimpse into the unlikely faces that will shape the future!

Louie Giglio
Visionary Architect/Director of Passion Conferences and sixstepsrecords

Don't read this book if you want to stay comfortable. This is a book that will challenge, exhilarate and sometimes scare you. It will encourage you to move out of your comfort zone and to believe that God can use anyone to reach into the most difficult situation, provided they are available to him.

In Philippians Paul encourages us to allow the mind of Jesus Christ to be in us. Patrick Regan has done just that. Step by step, his passion that others should know the good news that he loves has caused him to allow Jesus to invade more of his own life and to expand his comfort zone. How has that happened? Because each time God has asked him to step outside his comfort zone he's done it.

Above all, this is an immensely encouraging book about the power of Jesus and the good news to infiltrate and change the lives of the most alienated people. It is the story of a man who is honest about his inadequacies and his fears, but is able to say that God is bigger. It's a great story. Buy it for a good read. Read it and get ready to be part of a revolution.

Eric Delve
St Luke's Church, Maidstone

Patrick writes with refreshing realness about the highs and lows of living his faith in Jesus. This is an encouraging read for anyone thinking 'What can God do through me?' The short answer is 'All things' and the pages of this book are evidence of that.

Katei Kirby
Chief Executive Officer, African and Caribbean Evangelical Alliance

We hear sound-bites and see news-clips about violence in the inner cities. Many of us are appalled at the number of young people who've been stabbed in recent months. This book goes beyond the headlines to introduce us to the broken and hurting kids of today. Patrick asks poignant questions about the causes, and shows how compassion and the power of the Christian gospel can really make a difference in these young lives. An inspiring story that should challenge us all to move out of our comfort zone to reach a needy world for Jesus.

Rob Frost
Director of Share Jesus International

This book speaks with passion and vision about commitment to young people. It's about a young man's journey to reach and encourage a generation of youth.

Les Isaac
Director of Ascension Trust and Street Pastors

Anyone who thinks that one person can't make a difference needs to read this book! Writing in an accessible and easy-to-read style, Patrick (with Liza) tells his story with conviction and passion. It's an exciting and inspiring read that will help you realise that what you do with your life really does matter!

Malcolm Duncan
Leader of Faithworks

Patrick's book is the story of real life on estates in Britain today. Deeply moving in parts; deeply challenging and very inspiring. It would surprise me if you, like me, didn't ask yourself at the end of practically every page, 'What can we do?' God alone knows the answer to that, but, whatever it is, let's do it – quickly!

Sandy Millar
Assistant Bishop of London

This is not fiction, it's beyond an autobiography, it is a written revival! The author lives 3-D in a world of gun crime, gang culture and violence. This book is a wake-up call to the fact that our Western cities have become desperate mission fields. In his unique style, loaded with humour and sheer frankness, Patrick challenges us to jump feet-first into the Great Commission: reaching lives with the love and power of Christ. Health warning: this book is not for the squeamish!

Pastor Jonathan Oloyede
Gloryhouse

We live in an urban world yet few of us ever connect to the plight of urban, at-risk young people in our burgeoning cities. In *Conspiracy of the Insignificant* Patrick gives us a very human look at the pain and heartache as well as the joy and celebration of one of the world's largest cities, London. His insightful storytelling makes this both a challenging and a delightful read for all of us who know God is stirring up a new wave of the Spirit to impact our hurting world. This is an important book for all who feel called to be a part of what God is doing to make a difference in our world.

Tom and Christine Sine
Mustard Seed Associates

This really is a book worth reading. Patrick has been a good friend of mine for over ten years and so you would expect me to be biased. Which I am! But this book carries some vital messages for Christians and those who work with young people in inner-city Britain today.

The first message is that there is all the difference in the world between a comfortable Christian family and upbringing, and turning your faith and talent to real advantage. The second message is that change will not come unless you are genuinely committed to the people you seek to serve – individually, personally and by name. The third message is that, if you have the determination and the skill, you can motivate great numbers of others to help you, and your faith and commitment will see you through, even when the finances or practicalities don't look as if they're in place. And the last message is that, although of course we have a first commitment to those on our doorstep, there are places and people to be changed beyond our own communities as well. If the streets of South London and Trenchtown have less violence and gun crime in the future, it will be because of people like Patrick and XLP. If education prospects in Ghana are improved, it will be because of people like Patrick and XLP.

The media keep on saying we live in a hugely selfish, hedonistic and valueless age. This book shows that there are examples all around us, if we look, of actions that by God's strength are really changing our world.

Simon Hughes
MP for North Southwark and Bermondsey
President of the Liberal Democrats

Don't be fooled by this book's easy-to-read conversational style, because the message it contains is dynamite! The church in the UK urgently needs to rediscover a passion for the city and *Conspiracy of the Insignificant* provides the challenge to do this, encouragement about what can be achieved, and importantly clues about how to go about putting it into practice.

Fran Beckett OBE
Chief Executive of the Church Urban Fund

Conspiracy of the Insignificant

PATRICK REGAN

WITH LIZA HOEKSMA

First published 2007

Cover design by Wildfirestudio.co.uk

ISBN 978 1 842913 69 7

Survivor is an imprint of
KINGSWAY COMMUNICATIONS LTD
Lottbridge Drove, Eastbourne BN23 6NT, England.
Email: info@survivor.co.uk

Printed in the USA

Contents

Acknowledgements

Special thanks go to everyone who has helped write this book and has contributed to the journey along the way.

I want to say thank you to: Charlotte, for sharing your story and for your passion for those kids whom a lot of people have given up on; Kerry, for sharing how God brought you to us and what he has done in your life; Jason, for being so open and honest; Natalie Thomlinson and Val Kensington, for your insights and all you do which I guess can sometimes appear to go unnoticed but is so appreciated; Tim Powell and Leo Pswarayi, for your advice and input – you guys are amazing.

Special thanks to Les Isaac for mentoring me and reading over some of the chapters to make sure we got it right. Thanks to Simon Marchant for persuading me to do it. Special thanks to Mum, Dad, Becky and John for helping out with the bits I couldn't remember; I know Alan would have been proud!

Also special thanks to Liza for helping write this book – I have really appreciated your patience and commitment to the project; Mike Pilavachi for writing the foreword and for being a constant source of encouragement; and to everyone at Kingsway/Survivor.

Thanks to Simon Thomas, Mike Coates, Fran Beckett and Liz Biddulph for all your wisdom and friendship over the years. Special thanks to Maggie Morris who has become an XLP legend.

Everything in XLP is a real team effort; I have been so blessed to work with so many amazing people over the years, whose dedication and commitment to the cause have been incredible. Let's keep dreaming and trusting God for the future.

Patrick Regan

Dedication

To Diane, Keziah and Daniel

Without your constant love and support, XLP would not be happening the way it is now. You have always released me to do what I feel God has been saying, have made so many sacrifices over the years and have never complained. You're the best, I love you.

Foreword

I have known Patrick Regan and XLP for a few years now and much admired both him and the work he does. This still did not prepare me for this book. It challenged and gripped me in a way that I did not expect.

It is an absolutely compelling read. It has everything: stories that cause you to rejoice, stories that break your heart and stories that, quite frankly, made me very angry. Above all, they are all stories that teach. They communicate the truth of the situation in many of our inner cities and also the desperate need for the church of Jesus to wake up and rise up to be the good news there.

However, there is also the wealth of true stories of heroes who have been serving some of the most deeply marginalised and broken people in our nation with boldness and courage and, above all, perseverance. Church leaders who refuse to move to where it's easier, young men and women who literally risk their lives for the cause of the kingdom of Jesus, but also elderly women who have been faithful prayer warriors, in season and out of season. This is a book full of heroes. Wrapped around the stories is some of the best teaching I have found on so many issues around evangelism and justice, and all done in Patrick's disarmingly humble way.

I know Patrick. He is a friend. He is an ordinary guy who has fears as well as hopes, down days as well as up ones. He is the genuine article and he is desperate to see the kingdom come in his patch of London. Miracles are happening. Quiet miracles. Hidden miracles. Miracles in ones and twos. But miracles just the same. This great book tells the story and just by doing so invites you to become part of the story. This is a gem. Read it and be changed. I warmly commend it to you.

Mike Pilavachi
June 2007

1

Welcome to Reality

It had been an eye-opening week but nothing had prepared me for the world I was about to step into. Below Waterloo Bridge around 200 people had made their homes from cardboard boxes and old pieces of wood. Some marked their patch with a piece of worn carpet so they wouldn't have to sleep on the floor, others with just a dirty blanket that provided their only comfort against the cold nights. Men and women of all ages were busily getting on with their everyday activities; some stood chatting and laughing, others huddled alone trying to get some sleep, some sat smoking or drinking from bottles hidden in paper bags, lost in their own thoughts. Many looked barely out of their teens while others, particularly the men with their unkempt beards, looked like they should be in a nursing home, not living out on the streets. Possessions such as a change of clothing were stashed in stolen shopping trolleys or black bin liners, marking out each individual's spot. Dogs wandered around looking for scraps of food, some strays searching for a place to sleep themselves, others returning to their master's side with their findings. Occasionally a well-dressed couple or group would walk through, keeping their heads down as they made their way to the nearby National Theatre, their expensive coats and well-scrubbed faces incongruous with the scenes around them.

My senses were on overdrive taking it all in; I, like everyone else, had seen pictures of Cardboard City on the news but I'd never seen it with my own eyes. As the sun went down, groups gathered around fires lit in bins to keep warm, rubbing their hands together and chatting easily over the flames. It was obvious that this was a community of people who had been here a long time, people who knew each other, and we were strangers in their midst. Some regarded us with suspicion; were we students looking to study them or were we really interested in who they were and why they had ended up as residents in this infamous London location? As we got talking they relaxed and invited us to sit and join them, our circle only interrupted by a young girl, excited that she'd managed to beg enough money for a burger. We watched as the burger went from hand to hand, gradually disappearing as each person took a bite before passing it on. What totally surprised me – and to be honest freaked me out – was that the guy next to me, offered it up for me to take my share. I couldn't get my head around the fact that they had so little and yet were willing to share it with someone they had just met. I wasn't even sure what I was supposed to do; how could I take a bite of their food when it was all they had and at the same time how could I refuse? Would it look like I didn't want to eat something they'd touched or as though I thought I was above them? Head down, I took a small bite and hoped it was the right thing to do. When I looked up I caught sight of the words 'Welcome to Reality' sprayed in huge red letters on the wall. The burger caught in my throat. This was reality for the people living here, and for so many others living in poverty but it was like nothing I had ever seen. It was nowhere near the reality of the first 16 years of my life. I'd been living in a bubble and here, sitting with people who counted a cardboard box their home, who had no bed to sleep in, no money in their pockets, no place to wash and no clean clothes to put on, the bubble had finally burst. Some of those around me had nowhere else to go; for some living on the streets was actually preferable to the alternatives. I realised with a sickening jolt that having lived a comfortable lifestyle all my life I'd been completely oblivious to the depths of pain and suffering in the world.

***

In many respects I had a very easy childhood but my parents would beg to differ that it began smoothly. I was their first child and when I was still in the womb the doctors discovered that my blood type was different from my mum's. This was a major concern as if my blood got into my mum's system her body would start creating antibodies to get rid of me, so twice a month they did an amniocentesis to make sure everything was OK. They grew increasingly concerned and at 37 weeks decided they needed to bring on the labour as otherwise there was a risk of brain damage. As soon as I was born I was whisked off to the special care unit suffering from a high level of jaundice – as my dad recalls, I was about the colour of a ripe banana! The doctors warned my parents I was very ill and that they would have to change my blood (I'm still not entirely sure how they do that but I understand it's a pretty major procedure). The pastor of my mum and dad's church, Pastor

Anthony, came to pray for me and to the doctor's amazement the jaundice started to disappear. I spent the first eight days of my life in the special care unit and my parents were warned that I might be quite a slow child with little energy because of all that I had been through. They tell me now I was the complete opposite and was a totally hyperactive child!

Three years after I was born my little brother Matthew came into the world. He had only been in the womb for 36 weeks due to the same blood-related problems as I had and his lungs hadn't had time to develop properly. Though the doctors told my mum and dad to prepare for the worst everyone was still devastated when Matthew died just a few days later. Even in their heartbreak my parents were adamant they didn't want me to be an only child so despite the doctors' protests, Mum got pregnant again. Sure enough, at 24 weeks the same tests were done and the same problems discovered. This time, though, my parents had received a word from a friend in church that everything would be OK and they were completely at peace. There's no medical explanation for what happened but somehow my sister Becky's blood type totally changed while she was in the womb, completely eradicating the problem!

I think it was hearing stories like this from my parents as I grew up that meant I always believed in God and in the power of prayer. My mum tells me that when I was four she tried to wake Becky up from her afternoon sleep and found her cold and unresponsive. In complete terror she ran to phone the ambulance and came back to find me kneeling by Becky's cot praying for her. By the time the ambulance arrived, Becky was sitting up, smiling and giggling as though nothing had ever been wrong!

I've often wished I had a spicier testimony of how I became a Christian. Amazing as it was to grow up in a Christian home, it's easy to think that the story would just be a little bit more interesting if I'd really gone off the rails for a bit and had a really dramatic conversion. Truthfully, though, when I was about five years old I kept getting out of bed one night to ask my dad questions about the cross. After about the fourth or fifth time, I told him I wanted to be a Christian and that was when I made my commitment to follow Jesus.

My parents gave me a great example of what it meant to be a Christian. They both had pretty normal jobs, my mum being a hospice nurse and my dad being a welder, but they certainly didn't let that stop them from having adventures with God! They really took their faith seriously and certainly weren't going to confine it to church on a Sunday. Dad's always had good stories to tell, like the time he was welding a car for this bloke called Dick. Dick had just lost his job on a building site; he'd been stitched up and was furious about it. He was a big guy and Dad believed him when he said he was going to get a sledgehammer and take out the knee-caps of the people who'd cost him his job. My dad has no fear though and when Dick also mentioned that his back was causing him some pain, he didn't hesitate in telling him that God could heal him. Dick stormed off, slamming the door behind him, his anger answer enough. Dad carried on working on Dick's car and within an hour Dick returned and asked if it was really true that God could heal him. As Dad prayed for him, Dick felt what he described as electricity going up and down his spine, before he fell to the ground in the Spirit. Sure enough he was totally healed and came along to church, giving testimony to God's work in his life.

It was quite normal for Dad to come home with another story of someone God had healed or who had given their life to Jesus and, as a child, church to me seemed sometimes boring in comparison. We weren't seeing people get saved, in fact we seemed to spend a lot of the time thinking about ourselves and how we were feeling rather than those who didn't yet know God. So I took it upon myself to see what I could do and at the age of 15 my best mate, Pete, and I booked a 60-seater coach to take our friends from school to a Christian concert. The spaces soon went, but their enthusiasm wasn't to see the band, it was to come along and take the mickey out of Pete and me! We were under no illusions and prayed desperately that the band would be good – thankfully they were, and rather than everyone laughing at us, they spent the whole way home talking about how great it had been.

Although I was known for being a Christian, you could hardly say I was super-spiritual and ready with all the answers. When some kids in my class got totally freaked out about a Ouija board they'd done, they came to me for advice. They were petrified as the glass they'd been using had moved of its own accord, they'd thrown it across the room to smash it and it had just bounced back without a scratch. A few minutes later it broke while no one was touching it. 'What should we do?' they asked me. My reply? 'Don't do it again.' Which just about sums up my level of spiritual advice!

It was around this time that a new girl arrived in my school, fresh off the plane from Papua New Guinea. She was just 5′ 1″ and caught my eye with her blonde hair, bubbly manner and strange mix of accents she'd picked up from all the travelling her family had done. One of the things that made Diane stand out to me was that she really wanted to live as a

Christian, not just go to church on a Sunday but really make a difference with her life. Just a few months after meeting we were pretty much inseparable, sneaking out of our respective houses each night to meet up when we should have been doing our homework. I guess our schoolwork suffered but I consider it worth it, as just a few years later we were married!

When I told Diane in the summer after we got together that I was thinking of doing a mission in London, she was totally supportive. I wanted to try something a bit different from the festivals where I usually spent my summers and so applied to be on a '70 × 7' team run by Oasis in London. I'd been to the capital a few times with my family and seen all the usual touristy places like Big Ben and St Paul's but during the two weeks I was on the team my eyes were opened to a whole new side of the capital city. Mornings were spent doing Bible studies, then each afternoon we'd go off in different teams doing dramas, being part of street teams, running children's clubs and doing some door-to-door work which I hated.

We met loads of interesting characters with lifestyles and experiences that were totally outside my realm of thinking. In Leicester Square one night I met Annie, a well-built girl in her early twenties who wore heavy black make-up and hid her hair behind a bandanna. The large scar across her right cheek highlighted her 'don't mess with me' image. Somehow we got talking and I shared the gospel with her. To my amazement she prayed a prayer of commitment then and there, telling me the story of how she got her scar and why she was so desperately in need of grace. She'd been attacked by another girl, who had sliced at her face, so Annie had grabbed the knife and killed her, running to London from Sweden in an attempt to get away from what she'd done. The next night I met a guy called Michael at Piccadilly Circus – he was in his early thirties and looked quite smart in his black leather jacket so I didn't realise at first that he was homeless. As we got talking he told me not only was he living on the streets but he also had cancer; I just couldn't get my head around it.

As I spoke with each one of these people and many others like them, my heart began to change. My view of how the world worked and what life looked life was being radically altered even before I set foot in Cardboard City. But it was there that my bubble burst for good and my heart broke. I returned to the church hall we were staying in that night and prayed a prayer that changed my life. As I tossed and turned on my air bed, tears ran down my face and my heart was overwhelmed with the things I had seen. I'd never heard a sermon on God's heart for the poor but meeting people who were living in such suffering and poverty brought it home to me more than any talk could ever have done. I'd heard statistics about the number of people in the UK who were homeless or who had cancer but I'd never really spoken to any of them. Suddenly it wasn't statistics, it was people like Annie and Michael who made up these figures. There was no Hallelujah Chorus but there on the church floor I was suddenly intensely aware that all these people were made in the image of God and that as a Christian I had to respond in some way. 'God, I really want to see the world the way you see it and to capture your heart for people,' I prayed, little knowing where that journey would take me.

More than anything on that mission I learned that God's perspective was not the same as mine and that if I really wanted to see God I should look no further than the poor, the broken and marginalised. As U2 star, Bono, said in a speech to the NAACP (National Association of Advancement of Coloured People),

> God is in the slums, in the cardboard boxes where the poor play house . . . God is in the silence of a mother who has infected a child with a virus that will end both of their lives . . . God is in the cries heard under the rubble of war . . . God is in the debris of wasted opportunity and lives. And God is with us if we are with them.

2

Asleep in the Light

Although I'd caught something of God's heart, I think it's fair to say I hadn't at this point gained much wisdom or sensitivity. After the Oasis mission I went back to my home church in Chelmsford, all guns blazing that the church needed to get its act together and do something about all the people who didn't know Jesus and were living in poverty. I met up with Malcolm, our new youth pastor, and let rip at him. He was a great guy, really charismatic and down to earth; he saw my passion and just said simply, 'You do it.' I was gobsmacked. 'I'm only 16, you idiot, I'm too young!' was my immediate response. He smiled at me and said, 'I'll support you, help you and meet up and pray with you whenever you like, but you're now in charge of evangelism for this church.' I thought someone else in the church would realise this was madness but the leadership were just happy that someone was willing to take it on and didn't question my age or inexperience.

I persuaded about twelve others to get involved and help out and we started meeting up together to pray and worship.

We had some amazing evenings with a real sense of the Holy Spirit with us and people started to get really serious about following God. As our first step into evangelism we decided to do a week of mission in Chelmsford and run a non-alcoholic cocktail bar in the evenings to invite people back to. By the time the first night came around we were really pumped up; we'd been meeting with God and were full of passion to tell people about Jesus and couldn't wait to get started. We'd built a bar in the church lounge and put up lighting and a huge video screen in the hope of making it look cool and less churchy. At 7.30 pm, after praying, we turned up the music and waited eagerly for the first person to arrive. We waited and waited, getting restless as an hour came and went. I couldn't help but keep looking out of the door in case there were people just hanging around but the street was empty. By 9.30 pm there wasn't a smile to be seen among the team; no one had turned up to our first night and we all felt like we'd failed. At 16 it felt like the end of the world – we'd taken a risk and stepped out to do something we thought God was in and nothing had happened. I tried to be cool in front of the others but I was devastated.

As we started to think about packing up, something caught my eye at the window – a guy was walking past. I stuck my head out of the door to say hello and he asked what we were doing. I explained and he asked if he could come in. We sat down and started chatting and he told me he'd read about half of the Old and half of the New Testament and was desperately searching to understand more about God. Suddenly, here I was sat opposite a totally normal, intelligent young man who just needed someone to chat to about God. We talked and talked and before long he said he wanted to give his life to Jesus and we prayed together. The biggest party erupted after that – the night we had thought was a disaster and a total flop had led to someone becoming a Christian and we stayed up for hours dancing, singing and celebrating.

As well as the privilege of seeing someone give their life to God, it also taught me a valuable lesson. I had gone into the evening thinking it would be a success if we had loads of people show up and everyone said it was a great venue, but God told me clearly through just one person being there that he was calling me to be faithful. He showed me that success in his eyes is about being faithful to what he asks us to do and serving people because he loves them. I had been worried about my reputation and people thinking that I'd failed but the truth is that God would have been pleased with me even if the bar had stayed empty.

As a team we were really up for evangelism after seeing someone get saved and it set us up for our planned week of mission. We went out every day and did dramas, puppet shows and outreach on the streets and then invited people back to our cocktail bar in the evenings. All the nights were much busier than the first and when our youth pastor, Malcolm, returned from his holiday he said we should run it every week. So we started spending more time in Chelmsford, getting to know local people, hanging out with kids in the park and inviting them to our church evenings. We hung around quite a notorious pub and often ended up just looking after people when they came out after an evening's drinking and were completely wasted, staggering around and throwing up all over the place. One night I remember being in the park surrounded by a group of guys who were throwing question after question at me – all the classics about God, suffering and homosexuality. I hadn't read many books (I've never been the intellectual type) and to be honest didn't have any good answers for them, but I wasn't going to let that stop me. The more they gave me, the more I gave back until quite a crowd had gathered to hear us talking. Now I dread to think what I came up with but I was loving talking about God to people who didn't know him.

My passion for preaching about Jesus grew and I started to get invited to speak at different local churches. I didn't have much material so each time I just spoke on the cross, figuring that was all anyone needed to know about anyway! Diane and I wrote a 90-minute play called *Asleep in the Light* to try and encourage church members to wake up and do something with the love they had received from God. It went down really well in our church, where 300 people came to see it, and then we began taking it to other churches in the area too.

In the midst of all this I became aware of the terrible situation in Eastern Europe where war was causing thousands of people to starve to death. Even the helicopters taking aid were getting caught in the crossfire; the situation was desperate. Again I went to Malcolm and said that as Christians we had to do something. To his credit he didn't just roll his eyes at my latest passion but encouraged me to think of a way we could raise money. So we took over the church again and held a fundraising concert – we got a band in, set up a proper cocktail bar and charged people to come in, raising a few hundred pounds.

I loved everything I was doing. Every time I preached and someone became a Christian it gave me a massive high; when we raised money to send to Eastern Europe I felt like I was serving God well. But although I was confident enough to get up and speak or to organise an event, I actually wasn't a very secure person. I was only 16 and learning as I went and was struggling to keep the right perspective on what I was doing. Some days I would wake up full of energy and spend half an hour with God, reading my Bible and praying. Those days I felt like a 'Super-Christian' and would spend the morning walking on air, pleased with myself and feeling like everything was good between me and God. But other days, the alarm would go off and I'd sleepily try and open my Bible before dozing off to sleep again. I'd eventually wake up, too late to have my quiet time and rush off out of the house feeling really rubbish about everything.

I started praying about this and why I felt so low when I wasn't actively involved in evangelism. I spoke to Malcolm too and began to realise that I was buying into society's performance culture, that I was starting to get my sense of worth based on what I did for God. I felt challenged to slow down my activities and to take some time out but the idea confused me. I was serving God and following what I thought he'd called me to, why should I take a break from that when more than ever there was so much to do? I was receiving invitations to speak all over the place, I wanted to do more outreach and see more people saved and was desperate to encourage churches to get out and do the same. There were so many dire situations of poverty in our own country and around the world that needed money and support and pairs of hands. How could I justify taking a few months off?

It took a while before I realised that although there was a lot to do, God didn't actually need me to bring salvation to Chelmsford or anywhere else and that it didn't all rest on me. It wasn't that what I was doing was wrong but the idea of stopping made me realise that without all the work I was doing I wasn't sure I knew who I was. I started reading the story of the Prodigal Son and recognised something of myself in the older brother who had been slaving away for his father but in doing so had somehow missed out on a relationship with his dad. Like the elder brother, I was starting to feel that my worth was about what I did, not who I was. I feel really passionately that if we buy into today's performance culture we lose something vital in our relationship with God. God loves us for who we are, not what we do, but I for one get so easily side-tracked into thinking I need to serve more, pray more, read the Bible more and fast more in order to be holy in God's eyes.

It was a real lesson for me in understanding God's grace. Ever since I was young I knew that I was forgiven and loved but because I was forgiven and loved I wanted everyone to receive the same things I had and I wanted to serve God for all he'd given me. It was during this time when God called me to rest that I realised it's not an exchange and you really can't earn God's love. As Steve Hepden says:

> Christianity is both the hardest and easiest religion in the world. The easiest because we come with nothing, with empty hands at the foot of the cross. And yet the hardest for that very same reason, because our pride and selfishness does not want us to accept that we should come with open hands. We feel that we must bring something that we should contribute to our own Salvation, to be one who says we are in control rather than God.[1]

---

[1] Steve Hepden, *What Christians Should Know About Their Value to God* (Sovereign World, 1999).

I was getting my value from God through everything I was doing for him whereas God wanted me to stop so he could tell me he loved me anyway. For someone with my kind of personality – which is all about taking action and getting involved – it was a really hard few months to see things happening without me and to learn to sit with God and rest in him but it was vital for my character to grow. Life throws many tests at you that rock your identity so it's so essential to know who you are and whose you are; to know that God loves you whether you've had a good quiet time or not, whether you've preached well or not. Looking back, this time in my life always reminds me of the classic frog analogy that if you put a frog in boiling water it will jump straight out but if you put it in a pan of water and gradually turn up the heat it will stay there until it dies. Busyness is one of the killers of our intimacy with God and it's often harder to see it like that because it can be our expression of our love to him. Through taking a few months to rest, I learned some valuable lessons that would help keep me from burnout in the years ahead and make sure my security was in God and not in my own abilities.

I once read this fantastic quote in a Soul Survivor newsletter from revivalist, Duncan Campbell:

> These are days of much activity in the field of the church and mission work, but no amount of activity in the King's service will make up for neglect of the King himself. The devil is not greatly concerned about getting between us and work, his great concern is getting between us and God. Many a Christian worker has buried his spirituality in the grave of activity.

3

Mustard Seeds

When it came time to leave school I didn't really know what I wanted to do. I had been playing football for Colchester and had the opportunity to turn professional when I was 16 but I wasn't convinced that I was good enough. So I decided to go to a local sports college instead, thinking maybe I could be a PE instructor. I worked part time at a sports centre that was for children who were from difficult backgrounds and after a few months became the deputy manager. The longer I was there, though, the more passionate I felt about getting back to London and getting involved in one of the communities there. I saved all the money that I could while I worked and asked my church for support so I could apply for an Oasis gap-year course called Front Line. Oasis teams were going to London, Birmingham and Sunderland but I was adamant that I only wanted to be placed in London. Although it was a bit of a shock to the system, I wasn't even put off when, during my induction weekend, someone was shot in the newsagents across the road from the church we were staying at! Thankfully I was put in a team of four young people in Gypsy Hill in South East London and we all moved into a house together. I took one look at my new housemates and thought the whole thing would be a disaster. There was Nick who was very clever and into his computers and tekkie stuff; Anne was a health freak who didn't watch TV (and couldn't understand why I wanted to eat fish and chips in front of the telly!); and Emma who was so shy it felt like she didn't speak to us for the first few months. But we all settled in and started to find our way of working around each other, sharing out house jobs and getting stuck into our gap-year responsibilities.

Anne and I were placed at the Berridge Road Estate in Lambeth, and with a team of six others were to start a church. We made a motley crew as we joined our leader, Dave, alongside the Head of Strings from Dulwich Prep School, a couple of wonderful Jamaican ladies from the estate and another born-and-bred South London couple. Our church building was a small, empty shop fitted out with new carpet to make it less gloomy and, after we were commissioned by the Bishop of Southwark, we went to every house on the estate to invite them to join us the following Sunday. We started with about 30 people, some of whom had never been to church before – I don't know what they made of us as our worship was accompanied only by a violin that sounded more like a cat being tortured to death and some out-of-time tambourine shaking! It was great though – everyone was very real about their faith, there was no pretence and there was real integrity to the worship.

After my gap year at Christchurch, the mother church raised enough money to keep me on part time while I also worked for Crusaders as an evangelist. Two other evangelists and I went on a six-month tour that was packed out every night. It was a three-hour magazine-style show called 'The

Challenge of a Lifetime' which was full of competitions, video clips, large-screen computer games and live music. The idea was to look at different challenges faced at different stages of life and we'd take it in turns to preach at the end asking, 'What do you want to do with your life?' It was amazing seeing so many young people hearing the gospel for the first time and making a commitment to Jesus. Of course there were some interesting lessons along the way! One night, when we were near the Crusader's headquarters and the building was packed with 750 kids, the fire alarm went off just as I started speaking. For some reason I decided we should all stay in the building and I continued preaching while the alarm carried on ringing, but I stumbled over my words, petrified that there was a real fire and that hundreds of kids' lives were at risk. Usually by the time I came to the end and invited those people who wanted to become Christians to come forward I was pretty confident that some would respond, but this night I wasn't so sure. I was looking out at these blank faces; the only signs of life I'd seen were the odd glance towards the door in case flames were about to burst through and an understandable fear flicker across their features. Not exactly encouraging. I began to wonder what would happen if no one came forward – would I get sacked for not doing my job properly? Heart in my mouth, I made the invitation and waited with my head slightly down. When I looked up I was amazed to see about 250 kids streaming forward, cramming themselves into the space at the front, ready and waiting to give their lives to God! Humbled, I felt God reminding me that it wasn't about me, it didn't even matter whether a fire alarm went off in the middle, it was God who was meeting with people and changing their hearts, regardless of what I did.

In fact, there was a real temptation to get full of pride at being involved in a tour that was so successful. It carried a high profile, was sold out almost every night and was bearing a lot of fruit, but God put a longing in my heart to stay put in London and begin to really build something there. While the tour was amazing, I didn't get to know any of the kids, I wasn't involved in any of their lives and I never knew whether they carried on walking with the Lord or not. I wanted to really get stuck in and be around my church, so while I carried on working part time for them I earned extra money back at the sports centre I'd worked at when I was younger. I also went to Spurgeon's Bible College one day a week to study theology, as I knew that if I was going to be involved in speaking for the long haul, I needed some better foundations.

Everyone had warned Diane and me that if I did a gap year it would be really hard on our relationship and pretty much the kiss of death, as she would only be allowed to visit me one weekend a term. We weren't put off. Instead Diane would come up and visit other people in the church and I would just happen to 'pop in' to see them when she was there! So at the end of the year we were still going strong and wanted to get married, agreeing that she would move to London where she could start work for accountants KPMG as a team secretary.

The church gave us a flat to live in just outside the estate. Working on an estate in London (and living on its doorstep) was full of new experiences for me; I was so naïve when I started. When I was invited into people's homes I was confused by the fact that they all seemed to have rotting bananas in their kitchens. The fruit looked black and totally inedible until someone explained that it wasn't a banana but a plantain which is a staple in the African diet and that's how it's meant to look! I didn't have a clue about African history and traditions . . . I was completely surprised by their love of goat curry but willing to give it a try!

As the youth worker for the church, I got involved in the local primary schools, getting to know the kids until they all knew me by name and would regularly come and chat as I walked round the estate. The vicar, Patrick Whitworth, was great in that he would often come with me to meet the families on the estate (as they respected his position) but would then leave me to get on with things in my own way. I loved getting to know people but also found it heartbreaking to see all the problems that were suddenly on my doorstep. I was totally out of my depth and didn't have a clue what to do when I saw a young boy called David whose neck was red raw from his parents hands, or when I had my suspicions that two sweet girls called Janine and Sally were terrified of going home because their dad beat them. It was so hard to see houses with fist marks in the walls or parents who were off their heads with drink or drugs even while the kids were at home.

We helped in any ways we could and got Social Services involved where necessary but it was devastating seeing families torn apart. I felt completely clueless and learned like never before that I needed to depend on God and not on my own wisdom or strength. It's embarrassing to admit it but I think I was quite full of what I would have to offer the estate as their new youth worker when I started. After the success of the events I'd done in Chelmsford, I was expecting to come in and make a difference. The more families I met and stories I heard, I realised I really didn't have all the answers and certainly wasn't God's gift to the estate. There was no way I could solve all the complex problems and it was such a different world from the one I was used to. Even within the church there were all sorts of issues – like a lady who was looking after a mother who suffered from Alzheimer's and a friend of mine who had one daughter who got mixed up in the IRA and another who was on and off drugs.

As I walked to the church one day there were bunches of flowers laid in a small area nearby. I asked what was going on and found out that a young guy had been murdered on that spot. He wasn't someone I knew but his death hit the team and me hard. I felt gutted that it had happened on my estate and realised I had taken on a real sense of responsibility for everyone who lived there.

From that day on my language changed: I started saying 'we' rather than 'they' when talking about the residents. I felt a sense of ownership over the problems on the estate. I often think of it in the same way that if you own a car and it breaks, you're the one who has to take it to the garage – the problems of crime, violence and teenage pregnancy on the estate became my problems too. As a church team we didn't know quite what to do in the wake of this tragic death so we got the names of everyone on the estate from the electoral role and prayed for each of them, visiting every family between us.

It shook us up but made me realise more and more what our role needed to be on the estate. In Chelmsford I'd been involved in loads of big events, things we'd invited people to come to and now I was beginning to see that to be truly effective in a community you need to live and breathe that community's life. Sometimes with mission work, it's like we parachute into an area, do some work and then leave again. Even if we have the best intentions for this it can leave problems in our wake, pieces that have to be picked up by those who live in that area. It made me question what it really meant to bring the kingdom of God to a place; it had always sounded like a bit of a military term to me and I didn't really understand what marching armies had to do with anything. I started reading *The Mustard Seed Conspiracy* by Tom Sine[1] which talks about how the kingdom looks small and insignificant and yet, much like a mustard seed, it can grow from being barely visible into a huge tree that provides cover and shelter. As we struggled with how to be effective in a community that was reeling from a murder on its doorstep I realised more and more that we couldn't just put on events and invite people. We had to be the embodiment of the gospel and take it out to where people were. Like Jesus, we needed to walk amongst people, be a part of their lives and take ownership of our community and its problems. Our small acts did feel tiny, like mustard seeds, and we often felt weak in the face of such problems but we had to choose to remember that the things that would make a difference would be simple things like listening to people's problems, being loving and kind, and showing that we cared and were in this for the long haul. As Sine says in a further book, *Mustard Seed versus McWorld*:

> That has always been God's strategy – changing the world through the conspiracy of the insignificant. He chose a ragged bunch of Semite slaves to become the insurgents of his new order. He sent a vast army to flight with three hundred men carrying lamps and blowing horns. He chose an undersized shepherd boy with a slingshot to lead his chosen people. And who would

---

[1] Tom Sine, *The Mustard Seed Conspiracy* (W Publishing Group, 1981).

> have ever dreamed that God would work through a baby in a cow stall to turn his world right side up? God chose the foolish things of the world to shame the wise, God chose the weak things of the world to shame the strong.[2]

The issues that the community faces need to become our issues as the church if we want to be an authentic part of the community. So often we want our evangelism to be about the big and spectacular yet Jesus taught us that he cares about the small responses to his grace in our lives as we work behind the scenes. Many people believe that this world will get worse and worse and then finally, when it's really bad, Christ will return. I believe that God is interested in people's lives in the here and now and we have been commissioned by him to make a difference and to see our communities restored to the way he intended them to be.

Brennan Manning in his book, *The Signature of Jesus* says:

> A life of love lived unpretentiously for others flowing out of a love lived for God is the imitation of Christ and the only authentic discipleship. A life of service through the unglamorous, unpublicized works of mercy is a life marked by the signature of Jesus.[3]

It sounds so simple, and in one sense it is, but it's not without its problems either. When you become part of a community and take on its issues, those issues soon come knocking at your own door. In my case, it was seeing the anger and violence first hand. I was running seven youth groups at the time and at the end of one we went outside to find that it had been snowing. We all started running about, building snowballs

---

[2] Tom Sine, *Mustard Seed versus McWorld* (Baker Books, 1999).

[3] Brennan Manning, *The Signature of Jesus* (Multnomah, 1996).

and chucking them around, having a laugh. We were having a great time till I threw one that hit a lad called Chris in the face by mistake. He was 13 and had been a part of the youth group for a while without causing any trouble but suddenly things changed. He turned round and rather than accepting my laughing apology and retaliating, he gave me the fiercest look and began swearing and shouting at me. He reached for something in his pocket and for a minute, in the darkness, I thought it was a knife. I wasn't exactly relieved to see it was actually a spanner that he held up to hit me with. Thankfully a friend saw what was going on, grabbed Chris's arm and twisted it behind him to stop him before he whacked me, but at that moment Chris's dad walked past and thought we were hurting his son. He stepped in and, rather than Chris calming down, he totally lost it and threw the spanner, hitting me in the face. I was genuinely petrified at his anger and response and knew that I had to get out of there before he really hurt me. As I ran away he and his dad were screaming all sorts of threats – they told me to get out of London or they'd kill me; they had Mafia connections who would be coming after me. Knowing that it wasn't that unlikely, I didn't want to take the chance. I got home to Diane, grabbed some stuff, trying to explain to her what was going on, and told her we had to leave London. We drove back to my parents' house and stayed there for a few days, not telling my mum and dad why we'd turned up unexpectedly on their doorstep, as we didn't want them to worry about us living in a dangerous area.

It was Sheila Carter (now Simmons) who helped me to sort things out. She's the best youth worker I've ever come across and is one of my heroes. When you start working with young people it's easy to get side-tracked and think you have to look cool and like the same kind of music as them if they're going to like you – Sheila never bothered with all of that. In her fifties, she knew that wasn't what counted – she just offered unconditional love and, of course, everyone loved her back. If someone was in prison, it would be Sheila they called; if there was a problem at home, it was Sheila's house where they sought refuge. Likewise, it was Sheila that I phoned when I was terrified of coming back to London. She told me straight that I needed to face the family and said she'd come with me to help smooth things over. Sheila took me to meet the guy and I remember knocking at his door thinking, 'This is such a bad idea.' Sheila was quite calm and just said to Chris and his dad, 'This is Patrick – I believe you met the other night.' I stood there, frozen to the spot, but she explained the misunderstanding to him and somehow persuaded him that not only should he not get violent with me but that he should run a church football team!

Sheila demonstrated to me what it looks like to actually live the good news, and because Diane and I really believed that simple acts of kindness could bring change we tried to follow her example. We'd been spending more and more time getting to know people and they would always come and hang out at our flat, opening up to us about what was going on in their lives. We helped where we could with family situations and prayed for them. My study nights were constantly interrupted by different crises or just people wanting to hang out – and, to be honest, I never needed much persuasion to leave the essays and books behind to chat. Many of the girls would come over and, even from the age of 13, tell us that they were sexually active so I was more than grateful to be able to pass them over to Diane to chat to. Diane was brilliant with all the young people, getting them to rap about the estate as a way of expressing their feelings and listening to all their latest family, school and relationship problems. We really didn't do anything spectacular and it wasn't like we saw loads of them become Christians but we knew that God was asking us to invest in these young people's lives and just be there for them.

I was definitely learning my lesson that I just needed to be a part of people's lives and try and be a blessing rather than thinking I had something special to offer. If I was in any doubt, the kids would soon remind me. For example, I was asked to appear in a TV series called *Your Faith and Mine* which involved taking a strict Muslim girl to see what we were doing at church and then going along with her to her mosque and discussing the various elements of our faith. Loads of people saw the programme and were starting to stop me on the streets and in shops to chat about it, to the point that I was feeling like I'd become famous and my chest was starting to puff out just a little bit because of my newfound status. One of the lads on the estate, Ishmael, who was 15, saw it too – he was quite well-known in our area and all the other kids looked up to him in complete awe. When I walked past his house one day he was looking out of his bedroom window and said in a really loud voice so everyone on the estate could hear, 'I saw you on the TV!' I felt pretty good and my chest swelled just that little bit more, until he brought me back down to earth by adding, 'You were crap!'

4

'Jesus Was a Good Geezer'

Not long after we got married and Diane had moved to London, the vicar of my church got a phone call from a secondary school in West Dulwich. There had been a stabbing in the playground and the school was at a loss as to how to deal with the increase in violence among their pupils and was worried about their moral upbringing. They wanted someone to come and speak to the kids and as the youth worker it made sense for me to do it, plus I was well up for it, excited by the challenge it represented.

I thought about what to do for a first lesson and decided it would be good to look at heroes and role models. One thing I'd really noticed about the kids on the estate was that they were always looking for someone to look up to and so often their dads weren't around to provide a natural role model. For the guys in particular, this was a big issue as they would then look around for someone else to admire. Inevitably it would end up being the bloke who was a few years older than them who was earning hundreds of pounds each week through drugs and other crime and had earned the respect and fear of those around him. If your role model tells you there's no point going to school since you can earn more money illegally than you can spending years striving, then you can imagine what that does to your attitude to studying.

My first class was a group of 15- to 16-year-olds. At 21, I wasn't that much older than they were but the school felt a million miles from the one I'd been in. We'd spent hours at lunchtimes in the playing fields, getting all our energy and aggression out over a game of football, whereas here there was just a small concrete playground and nowhere else to go, even for PE lessons. I soon found myself in a small classroom standing in front of 30 kids who were all going completely mental. I just couldn't believe how riotous it was – the teacher was shouting but the kids were just ignoring him and it took him a full 15 minutes just to get everyone settled down so that I could start. It was pretty intimidating but thankfully they all loved talking about who they looked up to and why and so got pretty involved in the lesson, taking an interest and talking with enthusiasm.

The school were really pleased and invited me to come back to do regular lessons and assemblies. I tried to make everything as interactive as possible, having games, quizzes and competitions to keep them engaged and listening to what I was saying. One class I was in had three boys to every girl and was very rowdy; it was quite scary but I managed to get them talking about heroes. I asked if they thought Jesus was a hero and we talked about how 40 million Bibles are sold each year and how our calendar system is based around Jesus' birth. I asked why they thought that was and why we still celebrate Easter and Christmas. One lad stuck his hand up and said, 'It's 'cos Jesus was a good geezer, sir.' Before I had a chance to respond, one of his mates piped up, 'Nah, it's 'cos he got bust up on the cross, innit.' Even the hardest looking kids in the class were starting to pay attention and get involved, one of them saying, 'It's 'cos he came back to life three days later.' The first kid responded simply, 'Sir, that just leaves us with a choice.' I was gobsmacked! They'd just summed up the gospel in their own (unique) way in four sentences!

It was great getting into the classrooms and the kids and teachers were loving the classes but I felt like I needed to be in the schools more so I could get to know some of the young people better. I wanted to have a greater impact and do something less formal so thought that a lunch club might be a good way to start. I felt that to be able to cope with the things life threw at them the young people needed a sense of belonging and a sense of value so these were the things I wanted to work on and improve.

Despite the kids enjoying the lessons I'd done, I knew as a Christian there would be an inherited label for the club as being quiet and a bit boring so I determined to make the lunch club loud, exciting and the biggest and best club at the school. The venue was a little drama studio and I got four TVs hooked up to play videos (projectors were too expensive back then), had computer games and also did a bit of a 'God-slot'.

I was totally amazed (as were the teachers!) that each lunchtime between 80 and 120 kids would show up, running to grab their lunch as soon as the bell went so they could be first in the queue to the club. One ridiculously easy thing I did to help with a sense of belonging was to give them a pass to the lunch clubs. It was just a piece of laminated cardboard with a number on it but there was virtually a riot from the kids trying to get hold of one! This small token told them that they had somewhere to belong.

The group was much bigger than I expected so I quickly roped in a friend, Mike Godden, who was a youth worker at a local Baptist church and a couple of others to help me out. Over the weeks we looked at the things that Jesus taught and particularly his parables. We talked about issues of faith and of racism – a big subject for many of them. Lots of them with Afro-Caribbean backgrounds had grown up hearing about Jesus and were open to discussion but some of the others would tune out the minute his name was mentioned. We learned how to make the stories and discussions relevant to their lives to keep them interested, such as using the parable of the Good Samaritan to talk about the gang rivalry that was a part of their everyday lives.

The more time I spent at the school and with the kids, the more I was aware of how many issues they were facing. Violence had clearly become a problem, as the stabbing had highlighted, and there were regular vicious fights in the classrooms and corridors. One pupil started a fight in our lunch club and before we could break it up had cut his head open. Pockets of kids would hang out together in little gangs and pick on other children, even in lessons, and it was painful to see many pupils suffering from the effects of physical and verbal bullying. One of the overwhelming problems was that many of the young people had no sense of hope or future, and were without any ambition or aims in life. They knew as well as anyone that their school was notorious for low GCSE pass rates (9 per cent were gaining grades A to C whereas the national average was 50 per cent) and they accepted the fact that this would be their fate too. It tends to be accepted as fact that if you go to a failing school, you too will fail. Underage sex was common, with little awareness about sexually transmitted diseases and contraception, leading to an inevitably high teen-pregnancy rate. The teachers were under intense pressure – I spoke to some who had classes of 30, 18 of whom had special needs. All of those 18 really needed individual attention but there was no way that was possible even without having twelve other children who needed to be encouraged and stretched themselves. I noticed that a lot of the kids hung around in gangs, usually divided by their postcodes; so there were the SE guys who lived in the South East areas like Peckham and the SW (South West) gang which included areas like Brixton. These gangs are always portrayed negatively in the media as just wanting to cause trouble but I soon realised that not every gang was like that. For many it was just a place to belong, a group of mates to hang out with and a way to associate yourself with others by being in the same gang.

The London Borough of Southwark where the school lies is one of the most interesting and diverse boroughs in the country. For example, around 100 different languages are spoken in the schools there and the largest single ethnic group of pupils attending Southwark schools are those from black African backgrounds (29 per cent). Southwark is also home to a significant community of 'travellers'. Many of the young people were regularly drinking alcohol and I remember taking a lesson on the subject to address the school's concern about the pupils' consumption. We started with a quick competition to name different alcoholic drinks and one young person in a competition actually managed to name 40 different drinks in just three minutes.

It was overwhelming to see all these problems and barriers to these kids leading healthy and fulfilling lives, and easy to think that there was nothing we could do to change anything. Amazingly, though, somehow something as simple as a lunch club seemed to make a real difference.

'Billy the Kid' was one of the worst behaved boys in the school when we arrived. Most of his academic life was spent sitting outside the headmaster's office, and after school when everyone else was going home he was usually in detention for another fight with a classmate. Billy was hyperactive, had no self-control, would become violent at the slightest provocation and shouted and swore at students and teachers alike. He found it impossible to concentrate on his studies so was falling behind and, perhaps unsurprisingly, he didn't have very many friends. When Billy started attending our lunch club we knew about his reputation, having met him in the classroom. He lived up to it well, taking no notice of our requests for him to sit still; instead he would climb all over the furniture as if to prove a point. If he didn't win the competitions we ran he would instinctively punch the winner in the face to express his frustration. Over time and as we got to know Billy we began to notice some major changes in him as well as finding out what had made him so insolent and aggressive. It turned out he had been bullied throughout his school years and his parents fought so frequently and so violently he was often afraid to go home, even if that meant staying in detention. As we spent time with Billy, slowly his self-confidence grew; he was able to manage his anger better, became much calmer and started to get along with his classmates. His teachers were completely amazed when he started to apply himself to his work and achieved more than they'd ever imagined he could and attributed it to the strong relationships he had built with members of the lunch club team. It was so simple and yet it seemed to be working.

The more we got to know kids like Billy, the more we knew that they weren't likely to come to a standard church service. Their attention spans were just too short to handle a service and some of our traditions were a million miles away from their everyday lives. We needed to do something aimed at their age group, so a group of us from different churches in the area got together to start a monthly event called 'Sound Service'.

The service used multi-media to make it youth friendly and a worship band the kids could relate to. We had smoke machines, videos, competitions and made the talks as relevant as possible to their lives, addressing things like identity, how to handle failure, friendship and trust. We knew we were doing something right when one of the girls from school said, 'I never knew church could be like this.' Our aim was to show the young people that church could be relevant and interesting to them, not the stuffy, old-fashioned place they had expected. Even *The Times* newspaper came down and did a review on the Sound Service, their headline declaring, 'It's Christianity but not as we know it'. We couldn't openly advertise the service in school but if anyone asked more about what we were doing we could tell them about the Sound Service and many came along, intrigued to check it out. Somehow we began to get about 300 kids a month attending, and over the first year we saw 100 of them make commitments to God.

Two of the people involved in the Sound Service, Mike Coates (from the Ichthus Christian Fellowship) and Simon Thomas (a teacher at one of the schools where I was working), asked me if I'd be interested in moving to Peckham to start some more schools work. I jumped at the chance, increasingly aware of the need and of the difference we could make just by being there and serving.

Initially the schools I approached were sceptical about letting me come in. Their assumption was that, as a Christian, I would only be interested in taking RE lessons or assemblies to try and convert the kids and, of course, they can't let that happen in schools. Many had also had their fingers burnt by previous experiences where the assemblies they'd allowed Christians to run had gone down like lead balloons. As we talked I explained that my church and I were keen to help out in any way we could, in any lesson we could, and they began to warm to the idea. Our passion was to provide a more holistic package – rather than just sharing the gospel we wanted to be able to help the kids make wise lifestyle choices, whatever their beliefs. We knew that for the young people to avoid a life of poverty or crime they also needed a good education but the GCSE grades in the area were well below the national average. We knew we didn't have all the answers and didn't have a qualified teacher on the team at that point but we were aware that we could do simple things like taking half-hour slots each week to sit with a child and help them learn to read. The teachers weren't able to help all the kids who were struggling as their classes were so big but with these small acts of service we could increase individuals' confidence and give them a much better chance of doing well at school and beyond.

Gradually the message began to sink in to the headteachers and their staff that we just wanted to serve the schools rather than push our own agenda and we started getting invitations.

Some asked us to do lessons and assemblies, some schools just wanted us to come and hang out with the kids and play football or take an art class here and there. Others had particular issues they wanted us to address such as the use of alcohol or sexual health. We were amazed at how simple it would be for us to support these schools. The only problem was that demand began to grow so quickly that it was starting to become a full-time job.

We had no funding but Mike and I worked out that if we could get 17 people to sponsor us £25 a month, in addition to the gift from the church of £150 per month, we'd be able to go full time. We spoke to local churches and I went back to my home church to tell them about the needs and the opportunity for us as Christians to bring something of God into these schools. Peckham had a bad reputation and many people questioned whether it was a good place for us to be working but I was beginning to get God's heart for the area and was desperate to see it turned round. The same story kept coming back to me from chapter 7 of Joshua where Achan is found guilty of theft and is taken to the Valley of Achor (meaning 'trouble') to be stoned. Later, through Hosea, God promises he will 'make the Valley of Achor a door of hope'.[1] Peckham was well known as a place of trouble but I knew that God's heart was to find a way of bringing hope there and to see the kids' lives turned around. The theologian, Walter Brueggemann, once wrote: 'Hope is the refusal to accept the reading of the reality which is the majority opinion.'[2]

---

[1] Hosea 2:15

[2] Walter Brueggemann, *The Prophetic Imagination* (Philadelphia: Fortress Press, 1978), p.67.

We needed to believe that things could change, and to rely on God who is the only one who can change people's hearts and make a real difference. Of course that would give us problems with funding as many donors and grant-making organisations don't give to faith-based charities, but we didn't want to become just a secular youth work organisation. We were really aware that while we were able to help with things like reading and empower the young people to make good life choices, we couldn't change their hearts, only God could. We were willing to sacrifice easier funding routes in order to be able to have God at the centre of what we were doing.

Thankfully, friends, family and church members caught the vision and it wasn't long before we had enough money to get started; all we needed was a name for our work. Diane had a dream about what we were doing and about our vision to help the kids excel in all they did. We really wanted them to do well at school, to give them good job prospects, and for them to excel in all ways – physically, emotionally and spiritually. 'Why don't you call it XL?' she suggested after sharing her dream. Although I thought it was a pretty rubbish idea (encouraging husband that I am), I couldn't come up with anything else so we added a 'P' for project and the 'XL Project' or 'XLP' was born.

5

Restore the Streets

The more kids I got to know in Peckham, the more stories I heard that broke my heart. There are loads of reports about bullying in schools and Rakeem was just one teenager I came into contact with who was a victim of this. He was slightly on the small side, spoke only broken English and had very low self-esteem. The problem got so bad and he was so scared that at breaks he would climb a tree to get out of the other children's way and wait for me to arrive. As he saw my red Ford Escort pull into the car park he would climb down and run to me as he knew he would be safe when I or any of the team were around. For him the lunch club was a safe haven, somewhere he was accepted and protected from the misery.

Luell was just one of the many young people who we've seen acting as virtual parents to siblings while their real parents are out all hours trying to earn enough money to survive. I would see him cycling around Peckham, balancing his one-year-old baby sister as well as the family food shop that he'd just done. At the age of 13 he was responsible for so much around the home that inevitably his school work suffered and he would get in trouble with the teachers for not doing his homework and for being tired and inattentive in class. It was awful to see the cyclical nature of the problem – Luell would be unlikely to achieve much at school with no time to devote to studying and would probably end up also trying to scrape a living in difficult circumstances, maybe even leaving his own children in their siblings' care and therefore perpetuating the whole thing.

Others like Chantelle, on the other hand, said it was their greatest ambition to be a parent. At the age of 14 she was so hurt by other people that in desperation to find someone to love her she wanted to become a mum. 'I'll love the baby and the baby will love me,' she told me defiantly, 'I won't let no bloke get in the way.' It was terrifying to see how broken and cynical girls like Chantelle were and how easy it was for them to make their wish come true. They would soon find themselves pregnant and alone, realising how hard and isolating parenthood can be.

So many of the problems we encountered stemmed from children who were desperately in need of love and acceptance – which was exactly where the desire to join a gang often came from. We quickly saw that if one kid in a gang threw a brick through a window and the others said it was cool, he would keep doing it to win the approval of the other members. Some gangs are worse than others with their initiation rituals; many involve enduring physical violence such as repeated cigarette burns or cuts with a knife before you're accepted. One gang makes each member commit a crime before they can belong, that way everyone has a hold over everyone else and no one can go to the police. All of this just to feel approved and to have a sense of fitting in somewhere.

Again, it seemed crazy to think that belonging to something

as simple as a lunch club could help, but – combined with the respect we showed these kids just for who they were, and being there for them – it really did make a difference. For many lonely young people it was a place to be, even for the ones who didn't speak English and therefore had a hard time making any friends. They could come for the games each week even though they didn't have a clue what we were talking about the rest of the time.

In one school we had just four kids show up to our weekly club. We were getting disheartened and it felt in many ways that it was a bad use of our time when there were so many needs to meet elsewhere. But we knew that, as long as anyone wanted to come, we had to keep running it, so we simply determined to get to know the four who came. As we spent more time together we realised that one of them, Aaron, had a horrendously complicated home-life and was suffering some hideous abuse. For a couple of weeks he didn't turn up and we found out he'd run away from home and was sleeping rough behind one of the shops on the high street as things had become so bad at home. Another of the boys, Michael, wouldn't even make eye contact with us or speak to us but the teachers told us it was a huge achievement that he actually came as he wouldn't take part in anything else the school did. We kept the lunch club going, particularly aware that it was important to Aaron and Michael, and we knew that it was worth it when after about a year Aaron was able to look us in the eye and engage with me and the team. It's not a big and spectacular achievement but I know that Jesus wanted Aaron to know that people were there who cared about him and that boosted his self-esteem. The school was also amazed by the change in his behaviour.

The Bible is full of stories of transformation, people's lives being completely changed through encounters with God. People like the apostle Paul, who was once known as a murderer of Christians but became the world's greatest missionary, are a symbol of hope and of change. God can use and transform anyone – no one is outside his reach and his grace. These stories inspire me and spur me on when I encounter kids whose lives are so tough at such a young age – I know that things can turn around and I'm so passionate to see it happen. I want to instil in them a sense that they do have options, that they can make good choices and that they're not stuck in a cycle of poverty and pain. Although they may live in an area with a bad reputation it doesn't mean they have to behave in a certain way.

Peckham wasn't always the rough area it's now known to be. In Queen Victoria's day it was full of orchards and was the place people went from the city to get some country air. During World War 2 it was bombed and completely annihilated, after which it was totally changed. With a huge shortage in the workforce due to so many lives being lost in the fighting, the British government invited men to come from Africa, the Caribbean and Turkey to make up the loss. To accommodate so many people arriving at once, sprawling estates and high-rise flats were hurriedly built in Peckham. Many of the workers put in long hours to be able to send money home to parents and siblings, and stayed in England to have families of their own. Few of today's young people in Peckham were born in Africa or the Caribbean, but for many that is their heritage and history, giving them a sense of ownership of black history and culture but leaving them confused about where 'home' really is. Often in the schools pupils will say things like

'I'm from Nigeria' even though they've never been there; they're proud of their roots.

The new estates built after the War were difficult for the police to control and crime began to become the norm. I've often heard Peckham referred to as a 'God-forsaken' area; there were so many muggings that postmen and milkmen refused to deliver to addresses on some of the estates.

Lots of people turn up in inner-city areas and claim to have a hand in turning them around when really there have been people living, praying and working there for many years before. The thing that just about saved me from such arrogance was meeting so many amazing women in the churches in Peckham who had been passionately praying for the area for decades. One such woman was Val Kensington who said God had told her we were to ask for his blueprints for the area. We duly prayed and felt God said he wanted to restore Peckham and one of the things we should ask him for was houses to be built that had gardens. We and the churches of Peckham were really impacted by the words of Isaiah 58:12:

> If you are generous with the hungry
> and start giving yourselves to the down-and-out,
> Your lives will begin to glow in the darkness,
> your shadowed lives will be bathed in sunlight.
> I will always show you where to go.
> I'll give you a full life in the emptiest of places—
> firm muscles, strong bones.
> You'll be like a well-watered garden,
> a gurgling spring that never runs dry.
> You'll use the old rubble of past lives to build anew,
> rebuild the foundations from out of your past.
> You'll be known as those who can fix anything,

> restore old ruins, rebuild and renovate,
> make the community liveable again.[1]

Every week Val, together with a lovely Jamaican lady called Gloria and others, would walk round the schools in the area between 6.30 am and 7.30 am claiming them for God and his work. All of those schools, having known nothing about this, then invited us in to work with their young people. Val and Gloria prayed against dodgy businesses in Peckham's main high street and sure enough we'd see them closed down. Many shops were replaced with churches, and people say you're more likely to get saved than mugged on Rye Lane now! Estates that were prayed over have been replaced by the houses with gardens that God told us to ask him for. In many ways we know the favour we have found in the schools is down to years of faithful prayer from many people, some of whom we've never even met.

It was an important lesson to realise that in order to see real transformation in an area you have to work in partnership with others. There is not one super organisation or church or individual that is the sole answer to a community's problems. It's only when we work together, laying down some of our own agendas, that we can bring about real change. We spent a lot of time in the early years of our schools work establishing good relationships with the local police, local authorities and local churches.

While there were the highs of seeing God answer prayer in many different ways, there were of course a number of difficult things too. With money still tight I and a few others

---

[1] Isaiah 58:12, *The Message*

volunteered to do the 'Three Peaks Challenge', climbing mountains in England, Scotland and Wales for sponsorship. It nearly killed me but I was proud to tell Mike when he came to pick us up from Snowdon in Wales that I'd done it. In return he told me that we'd had the latest in a long line of break-ins at our office and had had most of our gear stolen. It's hard at times like that not to give in as you feel so fed up and angry. While we still had many of our original supporters, as the work grew so did the need for money to make it happen and, as any charity will tell you, fundraising can be a faith-stretching task.

We didn't always feel safe either. For a while Diane and I lived opposite an area known as Crime Mile. Someone had sprayed on the ground 'Walk past here and you're dead', but it was the route that I always took to walk our dog down by the old canal so I carried on. I have to admit I was pretty scared when I saw a whole gang of kids coming towards me. Even if they are quite young many are fairly big and strong and if they decide they want to prove how hard they are in front of the others, you know you're in trouble. I kept my head down, hoping to just get past, listening to them talking about me as they looked at me. Suddenly I heard one of the boys say, 'Don't take the piss out of him; he came and did a lesson in my school, and did this competition where you have to jump over a fiver.' I knew then that they'd leave me alone, although I also knew that it was best not to say anything but keep my head down, acknowledging the remark with nothing more than a grunt.

I was out of my depth in so many ways, learning about different cultures and trying to understand how to communicate across cultural divides. My dad had always taught me that effective communication was about stepping into someone else's world and seeing the world as they see it. You have to try to understand their experiences and where they are coming from, which is quite a challenge when you're from a white middle-class background working in a predominantly black Afro-Caribbean community. Often in a classroom I'd be faced with hostile faces whose expression said, 'What could you possibly know about my life?' It was intimidating and at times disheartening to think these kids had upbringings I couldn't even imagine, but I knew I wanted to find better ways to relate to them and certainly didn't want to be defeated because of the colour of my skin.

At times I felt it was a helpless situation but I was learning about true humility, acknowledging my dependence on God. I used to think that humility was about thinking you were rubbish at everything, but I was finding out it had much more to do with knowing you don't have all the answers. I couldn't solve all these problems I was being confronted with, but if I depended on God he could use me to help some people and that had to be a good place to start. I remember the story of Jesus and the blind man always used to confuse me. When Jesus asked this man who was begging, 'What do you want me to do for you?' I just thought 'What a stupid question – it's pretty obvious!' As I stopped and thought about it, I realised what an amazing question it was. In that culture the blind man was an outcast, and Jesus, King of kings, maker of the universe, stops to ask how he can help. This to me was such a picture of real humility and of what it actually means to be a servant of others. I couldn't go into these schools and onto the streets with all the answers, but I could offer to help in any way that was needed and wanted.

At first I thought that we were taking God into these schools, but I began to realise that he was already there and we needed to spot what he was doing and point it out to others. Floyd McClung in his book, *Holiness and the Spirit of the Age*, sums it up well by saying,

> Humility is first and foremost dependence upon God. It is God's human creation acknowledging its absolute and total dependence upon the Creator. Humility drives us past mere religion to a growing personal relationship with the living God.[2]

Often places like Peckham are described as 'needy' areas, and though I understand why people say that, we have to realise that every area is a 'needy' area, each just with a different set of needs. I soon realised that the reputation some people have given places like Peckham is very unfair. I find it a vibrant, exciting, colourful place to live – not the bleak, hostile environment often reported. There are some very complex issues which those of us who live there are very much aware of, but there are also some amazing people who are passionate about seeing people's lives changed for the better.

---

[2] Floyd McClung, *Holiness and the Spirit of the Age* (Harvest House Publishers, 1991).

6

Experience

As we got involved in more schools, received more invitations and became aware of more issues, we knew we needed to expand our team to be able to fulfil everything. By this point we already had five lunch clubs and were doing an evangelistic evening magazine-style show called 'Explosion' where we had seen about 50 kids become Christians. This led to a 'Just Looking' after-school club to answer questions from those who were interested in finding out more; we wanted to run Youth Alpha and other after-school clubs too. It wasn't only in Peckham we wanted to work either; we were looking to expand into more areas of Southwark as well as into neighbouring boroughs Greenwich and Lewisham. We planned a gap-year course that would invite young people from all over the world to come and serve for one or two years and gain a wide range of practical training and experience as well as receiving theological training. I was keen to get young people involved, aware of the risk my pastor had taken on me when I was only 16, and eager to let others have the same opportunity.

Since beginning the 'eXperience' programme we've had gap-year students from all over the country as well as from America and Canada. Some have gained such a heart for London that they've stayed working with us ever since; others have taken what they've learned and gone on to be evangelists, youth workers or to set up schools work in different areas of the country. It's been an amazing privilege to see people come and go, more often than not completely changed by the things they have seen and experienced. Kerry came to us 18 months ago and to be honest we weren't even sure if she would last the first week. She stuck it out though and has been an amazing example to me of the healing that God brings as we step out into his will for us and into serving others. I'll let her tell her own story.

While I was studying for my A-levels I got a virus and had two weeks off school. No big deal, or so I thought. When I returned to my studies I started getting panic attacks, felt weak and my body ached. Often I didn't even have the strength to stand up. I stayed off school for six months before trying to go back for just two hours a week, soon realising that even that was too much. It took a long time for the doctors to diagnose ME (Myalgic Encephalomyelitis, also known as Chronic Fatigue Syndrome or CFS) which is a little-understood illness, the main symptom of which is exhaustion. With ME you can have better hours, days and sometimes even weeks and one time when I was feeling better I went to church where I met a lovely guy called Dan. We quickly started seeing each other though often he'd come over to my house and I'd just apologise that I was too tired and would go to have a sleep while he waited downstairs. We stayed together over a few years and I eventually became well enough to do 16 hours a week as a receptionist but I would often come home feeling absolutely shattered. It was a lifeline to me, though, as I was so isolated at home; it was amazing to just be able to get out of the house.

That summer Dan and I went to a Soul Survivor conference and I was so excited that I managed to last the whole five days rather than having to go home to rest. I was, however, feeling really frustrated that I didn't feel like God was using me and complained to Dan that I wanted to get involved in something. That night Patrick got up on stage and told everyone about XLP and their gap-year course. I thought it sounded really cool to be able to do something to help these young people and tracked down the XLP stand that evening to find out more. I chatted to Tim, one of the team leaders, and got more excited about the work they were doing, at the same time as having a sinking feeling I would never be able to cope with the demands of the role. I'd never left home and, with having been housebound for much of the previous five years, the idea of leaving my mum and moving to London was completely petrifying. I lived in a tiny Wiltshire village where there were only 60 children in my whole school and just didn't know if I could cope with London and the crazy classes that Patrick and Tim had spoken about. Dan persuaded me to apply despite my reservations and I didn't think much of it. Even at the interview, I figured once I told them about my ME they wouldn't want me – I certainly didn't see myself as a safe bet. To my amazement, though, they accepted me and I had just a couple of weeks to get my head around the fact I was moving to London and was about to start working in schools.

The induction week was just hell for me. It was an intense training course where we did Bible studies, team games and practical workshops during the day and camped on the church floor at night. Everyone else was loving it and having a great time, but I couldn't cope either physically or emotionally. I was breaking down all the time, needing to go and rest and eventually moving from the church hall to a church family's home so I could get some proper sleep. Everything in me was telling me to go home. I wasn't cut out for this, I didn't think I could even be accepted as part of the team let alone do the work they were asking me to do. I missed out on so much of the team bonding as I had to sleep so often and felt isolated and on the edge of the group. Every night when I called Dan I told him I wanted to come home but he was amazing and just kept faithfully encouraging me that this was what God wanted me to do. Truthfully, I did know God wanted me at XLP, which made it very hard to walk away, but there were times when I was so upset I almost didn't care what God wanted. But somehow, after days of crying and feeling lost, I started to get really passionate about the vision for the year. A desire grew inside of me to meet the kids Patrick had been talking about, to work with them and convince them that they could do anything if they put their minds to it.

You'd expect it to be quite a culture shock from what I was used to, but I actually found it quite energising to be in such an exciting culture after my quiet village. I did find a lot of the kids quite tough as they were really rude and you have to work quite hard to earn their respect and to build a rapport with them. It was quite intimidating – especially as being 5′ 4″ I found many of them towered over me! Yet often their masks would slip and I'd get a glimpse of the real person beneath the hard exterior, which would encourage me to keep going.

For some it took a long time before we saw any difference, like Chloe who came to one of our after-school clubs. She is quite a well-built girl and very tough and at first she wouldn't even talk to me. If I smiled and said hello she'd blank me; when I tried to get her involved in things she wouldn't even acknowledge she'd heard me. After the best part of a year she'd opened up enough to speak to a few of us, although mainly she just told us she hated us or wanted to kill us! Bizarrely enough, that was her way of showing she accepted me (she was still ignoring most of the team). Over the last six months we've seen a huge change in Chloe, she even came along to Alpha. When I had the flu and needed to go home for a few days it was Chloe who prayed for me at Alpha – I couldn't believe it when I heard. Seeing her now, smiling, joking and chatting away, it's hard to believe she was so sullen and quiet at first – she even apologises if she says something rude to you – a far cry from her original insults and threats. I still don't know quite what made her so hard, I know things are hard at home but she hasn't told me what's happening. Maybe given more time she will, or maybe she won't, but it's amazing to see the change in her so far.

The eXperience course has been so rewarding but also incredibly challenging. During the induction week when I'd been told I would be leading assemblies I thought 'no way'. Even when they said, 'Everyone gets scared but everyone does it,' I just thought I'd be the first to not even try. The fact that I managed to do my first assembly in front of 300 kids and have since gone on to do loads more, as well as to preach in front of others, tells you what God did during this time for my confidence. I've also known so much of his grace and healing in that he's given me the strength to do my job and to complete the same hours as everyone else. It's hard to say you're completely healed of ME as it's such a strange disease but I can say that although I often get tired when I'm very busy (which is pretty normal I guess) somehow God has helped me through and I've done so much more than any of us thought possible. My self-esteem was always quite low and the years of isolation and not being able to do anything just increased that tenfold. God has now opened my eyes and I feel like he's shown me what he can do through me. It's not about me taking credit for stuff, just realising he can and does use me and that's enough.

He's also provided for me in amazing ways. Towards the end of my gap year I realised I couldn't bear to leave the kids. It seemed they had so many people in their lives that had walked away or let them down and I just didn't want to add to that number. The problem was that Dan and I had got engaged and I didn't know how I could arrange and pay for a wedding while still working as a volunteer. XLP agreed to keep me on, much to my amazement, and then I was further astonished when an anonymous donor agreed to sponsor me £500 a month so I could carry on in the schools.

Some days the work is really draining, both physically and emotionally. The kids can be hard work, taking their aggression out on you or playing up for attention. We don't always see the results of the seeds that we sow but we have to trust all the kids to God and know that our small efforts make a difference. Because so many of the young people come from broken and difficult family situations I'd love to ultimately combine the work we do in schools with working with the parents. I'd love to be able to support them too in order to see families restored.

It's been amazing to work in schools with XLP – I've seen situations that have made my heart break but also seen God changing young people's lives and giving them hope. God has done so much for me as I've served in this way and I'm so glad Dan persuaded me not to listen to my doubts but to go for it and to let God use me.

Charlotte was another of our gap-year students. She intended to join us for just the twelve months of the course, but things changed along the way!

When I was 21 I came to England from Denmark to nanny and work for a church, intending to stay for just a few months, but somewhere along the line God changed my heart and here I am eight years later! While I was nannying I was attending an Ichthus church and heard about XLP and their eXperience course. People told me to apply as I was interested in youth work but to be honest I was scared of kids work and even more terrified of working in schools. I didn't really want to do it but I applied as I wanted to stay in England and when I got accepted I just thought 'God, I don't have a lot of faith for this but if you want me to do this, please help me to take it from here.' On my first day I wasn't sure it was going to work – I didn't even know if I could get on with the team let alone the kids! Some of our team-building in the first week involved props like odd socks, frying pans, plastic cows, Marmite, mint sauce and marshmallows. . . It was like nothing I'd ever experienced before! One thing I was really looking forward to, though, was the theological teaching you get as part of the course from loads of great Christian speakers and teachers. Having come to faith at the age of 16 I felt like these sessions would really help me get a good solid basis to my theology and faith.

The schools were a different matter. To add to my fears, when I walked into the first school it was dark and dingy and I found myself alone in a corridor with ten huge black guys who towered over me. Though they didn't say anything or make any move towards me I was scared – I didn't even think I would be able to relate to these boys! At first I found communication really hard. Not only was I from a very different background from most of the kids, coming from a small town in a white, middle-class area on the coast of Denmark, but English wasn't my first language and it was a struggle. After a while, though, I found that it actually helped some of the kids relate to me as they too had come to England from another country and hadn't yet settled into the language and the culture.

I gradually relaxed into the lessons – they at least felt like a controlled environment, whereas the lunch and after-school clubs just felt like there were kids everywhere. I found it much easier when I was able to just sit and work with them in smaller groups and get to know them. When I started meeting the kids I asked God to break my heart for them and their situations and to help me to see them through his eyes. I'm not sure I realised what would happen but I started to see the depth of their emotional struggles and feel the pain of the injustices they were suffering. You have to be prepared for the consequences when you ask God to break your heart for a situation, and I felt overwhelmed by it all, but I knew that I just had to love them and to listen to whatever they wanted to talk about.

I was amazed at what some of them were going through.

One school invited us in to do a six-week creative writing course in their English classes with their Year 9 pupils (13- and 14-year-olds). We started with writing autobiographies and after a few weeks I noticed one quiet boy, Jake, hadn't written very much at all. I spent some time with him and found out some of his family background including the fact that he had nine brothers, eight sisters and four stepmums some of whom were in Jamaica, some in Manchester and some in Milton Keynes. I glanced over what he had written so far and saw that he'd been very close to his grandmother when he was little but she had died when he was three. Between the ages of 10 and 13 he'd lost his mother and sister to leukaemia, his cousin was killed in a motorbike accident and one of his brothers had been killed in a gang fight.

Understandably, the part of his story he was struggling to write was the good things that had happened in his life. Trying to think of something positive, I asked him if he'd ever been on holiday – Milton Keynes was as far as he'd been. We chatted some more and I asked him about his friends. When he'd been in primary school he'd had a number of good friends but none of them had come to the same secondary school as him. Of the four new friends he had made in secondary school two had since been expelled, one had stopped coming to school and the other had turned his back on Jake. Looking for some ray of hope I asked about his plans for the future but he told me he had no dreams or desires. I wouldn't give up and probed him but he told me his only idea was something silly. I told him I was really interested and promised not to dismiss the idea and eventually he confessed he wanted to be an inventor. His face got brighter as he described what he'd like to help create – a car that could fly.

His thinking was that there are too many cars on the road, too much pollution and too many crashes (like the one his cousin had been killed in) so he wanted to do something positive to combat those things.

Jake had the worst life I think I have ever heard about, losing so many people he loved in his short life, and yet here he was, when you probed to the heart of him, wanting to do something that would be positive for the world. He had a profound impact on me and the way I viewed young people; even in the midst of adversity and difficulty they still see some hope.

After the initial gap year there was no way I could leave children like Jake so I stayed on for the optional second year of the course. The kids that I had got to know were amazed that I had come back and kept asking why. When I told them it was to work with them because I wanted to see them succeed they were so pleased and it was a real breakthrough point as they began to trust me more. After the second year I still couldn't bear the thought of going and a position came up as Southwark borough leader. I had never seen myself as a leader and whenever I'm asked to do something my initial reaction is 'I can't'. But over my years at XLP my confidence has grown and I've found it to be an environment where you're encouraged and challenged to try new things and to stretch yourself. When I took the job I thought I'd only stay another year but I haven't managed to tear myself away yet – there's just so much to learn and so many amazing kids to work with it feels impossible to leave. There are certain kids I really have a passion for and I have told God that I won't leave until I have seen a change in them. They are some of the more difficult ones and I am not quite sure how or when the change will occur, but I'm determined not to give up on them. In their short lives many of them have already had family and teachers give up on them, and so they don't need me to bail out on them as well.

One of the things I love about doing the clubs is that we can help people who are lonely to find a place to belong and sometimes do a bit of friendship matchmaking. At the start of a certain lunchtime club I would go out around the school and look for anyone on their own to invite. This one boy, Billy, was always hiding in the same spot, alone on a bench, but would come to the club when I invited him. He struggled to make friends and was scared of one of the other boys who came to the club, so he'd wait for me to go and get him before he'd come in. We also found another boy who was a bit of a loner and got them talking; now they're really good friends and hang out together all the time. Anyone who's known the loneliness of not having friends at school will know what a difference it makes to have someone to hang around with – all we did was provide a way for them to meet and get to know one another.

One of the boys in Year 7, Giovanni, was the most difficult child I'd ever come across and was a real challenge for me to work with. He would annoy everyone, start fights for no reason, wouldn't follow instructions and would be rude to anyone and everyone. It got to the point where I didn't want him to come to the club any more as he caused so much trouble and made life so hard for everyone. It was only at this point that I decided to pray for Giovanni and ask God to help me to see him through his eyes. I started to talk to him each week and gradually began to get to know him and to hear about his family and his life. We often talk to the kids about their hopes to get them thinking about the future and how they could fulfil their ambitions. When I said to Giovanni, 'What do you want to do when you leave school?' he just shrugged his shoulders and sank deeper into his chair. 'It doesn't matter,' he said. 'Of course it does,' I replied. He shook his head, 'Mum says I'll never make it. She says I'll either end up in prison like my brother or a gang leader like my cousin.' It took me ages to persuade him it was worth telling me what he was interested in and he eventually said he'd thought about being an accountant. I encouraged him to make an effort with his school work to get his qualifications and especially to try in maths. We talked about how it was important for him to stay in the school system and that to do well he needed to change his attitude and not to lose his temper with the teachers.

Over time, Giovanni and I built a good relationship and he began confiding in me about things going on in his life. One day I heard him boasting to his friends about sleeping with a girl, then he came over and said, 'What do you think about what I just said?' I told him that I thought that at 13 he was very young to be having sex but that he needed to make sure he and the girl were protected if he did. As we talked he admitted that he hadn't actually done any of the things he was claiming he had, so I asked why he'd said it. 'I wanted to see how you'd react,' he said simply. He was testing me to see if I would reject him if he did something he knew I didn't approve of. When he saw that I hadn't he opened up to me in new ways and we had great conversations. Unfortunately, now, two years on, he's become involved in a gang and is avoiding me. He knows what he's doing isn't right and that's why he doesn't want to see me, but I still pray for him. He has an amazing influence and authority over his peers and I get so excited to think about the impact he could have if he used that influence for good instead of getting into trouble.

As well as the young people, I've also loved working along-side some of the teachers too. We've come across a number of Christian teachers working in schools who are desperately in need of some support and encouragement and it's fantas-tic to be able to be there for them too. One woman I've become good friends with is Natalie who is the pastoral leader at one of the schools in my borough. She works to help kids in some really tough situations, like one girl who recently tried to commit suicide. Between us we were able to talk to the girl, her friends and her family and try to support them through this very difficult time. We meet up weekly to talk about and pray for her students and have seen many answers to prayer. The young people she is working with are in seriously difficult circumstances and dealing with gang issues and teenage pregnancies, are in trouble with police, have suffered sexual and physical abuse and so much more. She talks to them and does everything she can to help them, and I try to support her and her students as best I can. Often I feel out of my depth and I constantly have to remind myself to trust that God has put me here for a reason.

While I've been working with these young people God has done so much in me too. My self-esteem hasn't always been great but it's definitely getting better and I've done things I would have never thought possible. The eXperience course and working with XLP has changed me so much. While it can be challenging and hard work to work with young people, particularly those who are struggling in so many ways, it also feels like a huge privilege too. XLP is a crazy mix of people, but the one thing we all have in common is a passion for young people and to see God move in their lives so that they can know their true worth. If I can help them to realise that, I'll be more than happy.

7

Cultural Clash

'Will you two just be quiet?' I shouted. I liked to think I was pretty good at controlling a class and keeping them quiet without resorting to raising my voice but on this particular day I was losing it. While I was trying to conduct a lesson on peer pressure, two boys behind desks at the back were hunched over, constantly whispering to one another. They'd been this way ever since I started and I'd had enough. 'Sorry sir,' one replied quietly. 'I'm just translating what you're saying for my friend so he can keep up. He doesn't understand any English.'

That shut me up! In many classrooms this could be a good line to get away with chatting to a friend for an hour, but here in Peckham I knew it to be true. One of the schools we worked in had 65 mother-tongue languages – 65 in just one school! Often the kids spoke English but many of their parents didn't, so you'd get these bizarre situations with young people being told off by the head and having to translate to their mum or dad what was being said.

Sometimes even the English expressions the young people used seemed like a different language to us. The West Indian kids would say things like 'I ain't skinning no teeth with ya' and it took me a while to work out that they meant 'I don't want to talk to you'. There were so many cultural differences to get used to. I'd been amazed when I'd first come to Peckham that it was the only place I'd ever seen where you could buy a goat and a mobile phone in the same shop! That was nothing compared to some of the challenges we faced in understanding where many of the kids were coming from. Two boys we worked with were from Sierra Leone. One had a bullet still lodged in his skull where he had been shot as he and his family fled; the other, at the age of 18, still slept in his mum's bed on Guy Fawkes Night as the fireworks reminded him too much of the sounds of war he'd heard back home. A kid called Ibrahim from Sierra Leone told us about his horrendous experiences as a child soldier.

In terms of religious differences you had to tread very carefully too – if you asked a class who they most feared, some of the kids from Asia or Turkey would immediately say Allah. You couldn't talk about God as a father to them, as it was so outside their realm of thinking and offensive to the things they had been brought up to believe. Teachers would ask us for our help and opinions on things like parents taking their kids back to Morocco for abortions, or how we thought they should tackle the issue of the illegal female circumcisions they knew were taking place. This wasn't the kind of stuff you could read in the average schools work manual!

When I first started schools work I was so ignorant about black history and culture. To be honest, I didn't even know how black people had come to be in this country. The only black person I knew very much about was Martin Luther King and so I used to do a lot of lessons on him. He was such an inspirational man in so many ways but one of the things that always stood out to me was his ability to persevere. When he was born, black people had to give up their seats on the bus to white people. Black churches were burnt to the ground by the Ku Klux Klan who terrorised whole communities and left dead bodies hanging from lampposts.

Martin Luther King wasn't beaten by all of this violence and degradation or his people's history of being continually downtrodden and abused. King's passion for justice was stronger than all of that. I'm sure you've seen the images of the marches he led: men and women peacefully protesting their rights to be equal meanwhile being set upon by dogs, being flattened by huge water hoses, being beaten and abused at every turn. The thing I love to remember is how every time someone was struck down they would pick themselves up, dust themselves off and carry on.

The tests in my life have been nowhere near as hard, but often when XLP have been short on money again, or another kid who has been making real progress gets into a fight and gets kicked out of school, I can feel like giving up. It really helped to remember Martin Luther King and his ability to keep going because of what he believed in. He sometimes received up to 50 death threats a day telling him to stop what he was doing, and people tried to petrol-bomb him time and again, but nothing dissuaded him from what he knew God called him to do. In fact it was one night when he received another phone call threatening his life that King's faith became real to him. He was full of fear for the lives of his family and feeling totally weak, and that was when he cried out to know God for himself. I love the honesty of the prayer that he prayed and the promise from God he received in reply. This is an extract from one of his sermons:

> I got to the point that I couldn't take it any more. I was weak . . . And I discovered then that religion had to become real to me, and I had to know God for myself. And I bowed down . . . I will never forget it . . . I prayed a prayer and I prayed it out loud that night. I said, 'Lord, I'm down here trying to do what's right. I think I'm right. I think the cause we represent is right. But Lord, I must confess that I'm weak now. I'm faltering. I'm losing courage.' And it seemed at that moment that I could hear an inner voice saying to me, 'Martin Luther King, stand up for righteousness. Stand up for justice. Stand up for truth, and lo, I will be with you, even until the end of the world.' . . . I heard the voice of Jesus saying still to fight on. He promised never to leave me, never to leave me alone. He promised never to leave me, never to leave me alone.

My ignorance and the multi-cultural nature of the schools we worked in inspired me to learn more about black history and how Peckham came to be the multi-cultural place it is. It also caught my attention that in 1 Chronicles 12:32 it says that the men of Issachar 'understood the times and knew what [they] should do'. This hit home to me that if I wanted to communicate effectively in these schools and communities I really needed to understand where the young people were coming from. I didn't want to just dip into a bit of culture; I knew that I had to give 100 per cent to do it well.

Les Isaac, a larger-than-life character and a member of the Ichthus church, heard what I wanted to do and said he would help me. Les and his family came to England from Antigua when Les was seven, and he grew up in Islington. At school he got called 'golliwog' and 'nigger', often being beaten up by bigger white boys. In response, Les became very aggressive and it wasn't long before he had the reputation as one of the best fighters in his school, always keeping a knife in his pocket. He started to smoke ganja and to hang out with Rastafarians who believed that white people were the oppressors and the allies of Satan, while black people were God's chosen ones.

Les's mother died when he was 17 and he started to question whether there was more to life than he was experiencing. Late one night he bumped into a preacher in a café and the gospel story became real to him for the first time. From that moment on he hasn't stopped telling people about Jesus and he now runs a fantastic project called Street Pastors. They engage with people who are on the streets in urban areas late at night, often as they have come out of clubs and bars and are in need of a little help. He is also Director of the Ascension Trust who work in both the UK and Africa helping many living in poverty. To help me get a better understanding of black culture, Les said I should do a mission trip to Ghana, from where many of the young people in Peckham are descended.

Like many people, my only experience of Africa was seeing starving children on the TV so I didn't really know what to expect. At the last minute Les had some things he needed to sort out in London so we (a team of 16 young people from churches in south east London) went on ahead and he said he hoped to join us after the first week. It felt even more daunting without him there, but when we arrived in Accra (Ghana's capital) for our induction week, we couldn't have been made to feel more welcome. Over 40 people from the church turned up to welcome us, they shouted out my name (as I was the team leader) and sang to us the song 'I Love You With the Love of the Lord'. It was a very strange experience in the middle of a busy airport!

It took us a while to get used to the 32-degree heat which

was more intense than anywhere I'd been before. Everywhere we went children shouted 'Aubruni!' meaning 'whitey', and tried to touch you. It was quite overwhelming and strange to be the centre of attention just for being white. One of the first things we did was some open-air evangelism in a market-place. We did sketches and dances and invited people to come for prayer if they wanted to know Jesus or would like healing. The response was like nothing I have ever seen in England. About 35 people wanted to make a commitment to Jesus and about 50 more wanted prayer for healing – anything from diarrhoea and malnourishment to malaria.

After our week of team building, prayer and preparation for what lay ahead we were commissioned by the church members and headed off to a village called Abeka. It felt like being in a film as we travelled miles over dusty red soil, with not even a track mark to distinguish a path for cars. When we arrived in Abeka we saw small huts grouped together, three or four forming a courtyard between them. Families of seven people would all sleep in one room together, on thin mattresses that barely covered the hard floor. Though the villagers lived in extreme poverty they were incredibly generous to us and fed us huge meals. We couldn't help but feel guilty that a lot of the time we were struggling to finish them. One time when our hosts had made us a huge bowl of rice pudding for breakfast we knew that no matter how much we tried we just couldn't get through it and the pastor took it outside and clapped his hands. Within just a few seconds a group of six children fell upon it, spoons in hand and devoured it.

One of the most important historical sites Les wanted us to see was Cape Coast Castle (also known as Slave Castle) which stands a few hours' drive from the capital on Ghana's beautiful coastline. The whitewashed buildings seemed innocent enough, until we stepped inside and learned of the horrific history contained inside their walls. This was the place where slaves were kept, often for months at a time, before being shipped off to America or the Caribbean. As we walked inside into a tiny dungeon below ground that would struggle to hold 150, it was barely possible to believe that a thousand men had at one time crowded into this space. Day and night they were left here, without light or air, their only relief 30 minutes a day to walk in the courtyard. Inside there was no place to go to the toilet; they were forced to go where they stood and over the 200 years of this practice, their waste raised the floor level by two feet. Some were starved, others chained to the walls, their scratch marks still visible on the walls. Those who died were unceremoniously dumped in the sea.

Another similar dungeon at one time held 500 women and young girls who awaited the same fate as their male counterparts. Survivors of both sexes were eventually stripped naked and forced through what was known as the 'door of no return' – a dark, narrow tunnel which led to the beach, down a stone ramp and onto a waiting ship. Off they would set for the Caribbean or America, the conditions on the ships in many cases even worse than in the castle. It was a horrifying experience just seeing the conditions thousands were forced to live and die in, and it was impossible to imagine how horrendous life was for them. They were wrenched from their homes and families, dragged to Cape Coast Castle, then left to rot for a few months before being packed like sardines onto a slave ship where between a quarter and half of them would die before reaching their destination. For those who did survive, all the future held was life as a slave, exiled from their family. Estimates of the number of slaves transported from Africa vary from 12 million to 25 million. One estimate says that in 1700, at the height of the slave trade, more than 650,000 slaves were exported in that year alone.

As we came out of Slave Castle, blinking in the bright sunshine, I struggled to get my head around all that I had just seen and learned. I looked around the coast and someone pointed out that one of the first British churches that had been built in Ghana was built above the dungeon. Rather than this being a comforting sight it was sickening to realise that the members of this congregation would have sung their songs about a God of love while their fellow man rotted just a short distance away. It was horrifying to think they had been a part of this injustice and so many despicable acts. As I spoke to Les, who had by now joined us, he pointed out that there were also white Christians who sold themselves into slavery in order to set black slaves free; you could only hope that if you had been around in those times you too would have been willing to take such a sacrificial stand against the view that selling black men and women into slavery was all right.

Despite its history, Ghana is an amazing country. It is Africa's second largest producer of gold and supplies 15 per cent of the world's cocoa. It should be well off but instead it suffers terrible poverty because of corrupt governments in the sixties and seventies. There's actually enough food for everyone to eat but it doesn't get to people because of a lack of infrastructure. It was devastating to see fields where the plantains rotted away as there was no one there to collect them, having just left children whose stomachs had popped and become protruding because of lack of food. Near the village we saw electricity pylons but there was no money to connect the people to this vital supply that would make their lives so much easier. The vast majority of people living there go to church each week because it is a cultural thing and not because they have an intimate relationship with God. They were really open to the things we had to say, especially when we talked about embracing the kingdom of God and what that might mean for Ghana. We also spoke about how God longs to know his children in an intimate way and how intimacy with God and involvement in society should always go hand in hand.

Les introduced us to an amazing Christian woman, Pastor Akousa, who works in the Ashanti Akim communities and has set up a charity called AACO (Ashanti Akim Community Organisation). She is passionate about helping the people of Ghana to help themselves and rightly believes that as Christians we should be the answer to the poor communities and look after our less fortunate brothers and sisters. She told us that yes the communities in Ghana needed water and health care facilities but their biggest barrier to long-term change is a lack of education. She introduced us to loads of families with similar stories of poverty preventing them from sending their children to school. We met kids like Steven who at the age of eleven had lost both his parents and was now living with his grandmother. She couldn't afford to send him to school, though the English equivalent would be just £2 a term, so he spent his days hanging around and doing nothing. What hope did he have for his future? Or another Steven, who was eight, whose father had been involved in an affair which led to his birth. He was given to his grandmother to look after but when he was seven she died and so his aunt began to take care of him. With children of her own she wasn't able to afford the fees to send him to school; it was a sacrifice to find the food to feed him.

We saw other groups of young children hanging around and we asked why they weren't in school. Members of the local community told us that the schools aren't built to last so when a storm comes, the roofs fall in and the place becomes unusable. There isn't the money for the kids to travel elsewhere so they have to wait for the school building to be sorted out before they can return to their education. Sometimes this can take months. We soon made sure that both Stevens got sponsored, and they are both doing really well at school. It's amazing and humbling how an insignificant amount to us like £2 can change someone's life.

For the lucky ones who do go to primary school, their education is still short-lived. As soon as they are at an age when they can be useful in the working world they are sent to the fields or to sell things at market. There's little hope of a decent education and good job prospects so they know they will end up struggling like their parents. They can't get good jobs, they get bored, they get drunk, they sleep around and inevitably teenage pregnancies are numerous. Just like in the parts of South East London we were working in back home, there was little ambition and hope among the young people. It was equally heartbreaking.

Even as we were leaving Ghana I wanted to go back – they were such warm and generous people, so welcoming and so thankful for anything we were able to do. The same vision burned in me for Ghana as it did for London: I wanted this place of trouble to become a place of hope. Once I'd seen the needs there I knew we couldn't just turn away, we had to come back regularly and do something.

8

Back to Africa

Each year since our first visit to Ghana we have returned there, usually with our eXperience students, as we believe not only do they have a lot to give, they can also learn so much from seeing these problems and meeting these amazing people themselves. As well as going back to Accra we have also spent time travelling to villages hours away from the capital, places where aid rarely reaches. We have visited schools, hospitals and churches as well as doing open-air presentations with dances, sketches, puppets and gospel stories.

But soon we began to get passionate about doing more. The more poverty you see the more you're aware you can't change everyone's lives, but God kept reminding us that we could do *something*; we could even change a whole village. An idea formed in my mind and I spoke to Pastor Akousa about it. 'How much would it be to build a secondary school here in Danpong?' I asked her. Her estimate was about £30,000 for a facility that could provide an amazing secondary school with three large classrooms, an assembly hall and even have a much-needed health clinic attached to it. There were hundreds of villages in the Ashanti Akim district but only three secondary schools. The team and I came back to England desperate to raise the money to make it happen. That year I was leading the youth work at Spring Harvest and when I shared about the poverty in Ghana and the need for a secondary school to give the kids there a future, I was blown away that in the collection we received £21,000 from the young people. We also spoke in churches and that resulted in individuals starting to give; one of our supporters even ran the London Marathon to raise some money.

When we went back to Danpong to let them know they would soon have a secondary school, we met with the chief of the village and his elders. They were overwhelmed and shocked. They couldn't work out why this predominantly white team would want to come back to their village year after year and not only come back but help build a school. One of the chief elders was a witch-doctor who wanted to come and pour some spirits over the land and do some kind of ceremony. We said we would rather just pray for it if he didn't mind! That night we gathered the whole village to explain what was going on, and I preached on the word 'hope' again. God's Spirit really moved on people and we spent hours praying for all those who responded.

On that same trip we spent some time in Juaso, where we did an open-air event and as usual loads of people came up for prayer. One woman who had been crippled for years with back pain began to jump around and shout that she'd been healed. I was trying to pick my jaw up off the floor and pretend that I really was a man of faith who had totally believed God would grant him the healing he'd asked for, but I think I was even more surprised than she was! As I was recovering, one of the team came over, telling me how they'd just seen a man healed from a breathing problem. We were all blown away and it felt like being on cloud nine seeing God do the miraculous right before our very eyes.

Then the mother of a small boy pressed through the crowd. She placed her son in my arms and asked me to pray. He was totally malnourished, he weighed hardly anything and his arms were so thin they were about the thickness of just a few of my fingers. I prayed, but I knew we also needed to get him to a hospital as quickly as we could. Sure enough, when we arrived there they told us he would have died if he had waited any longer.

I went home that night devastated. We'd seen God heal people but had also come face to face with a boy dying from lack of food. Haunted by his sunken eyes, hollow cheeks and emaciated body, I cried out to God, trying to make sense of this and asked the local pastors there how they handled it when such senseless death surrounded them on a daily basis. They told me all they could do was hang onto the fact that one day every tear will be wiped away. 'One day you'll meet that boy in heaven,' they said. 'You might not recognise him, though, as he'll be laughing and running and so happy. Until that day you have to just do what you can.' I've had to cling to that many times when faced with appalling poverty and pain, not least when I heard that the same boy had died six months later from malnutrition.

The reality of going somewhere like Ghana is that you are faced with death and disease, poverty and pain, everywhere you go and you have to be able to give it all over to God or the weight of the pain will keep you from being able to do anything. As the Ghanaian pastors suggested, it helped to cling to the words from Revelation 21:3–5:

> And I heard a loud voice from the throne saying, 'Now the dwelling of God is with men, and he will live with them. They will be his people, and God himself will be with them and be their God. He will wipe every tear from their eyes. There will be no more death or mourning or crying or pain, for the old order of things has passed away.'

Until that day comes when God's order is fully restored we must get on with doing the work of his kingdom, which includes trying to get rid of some of the pain that exists now. This means reaching out to the poor, the broken and the marginalised and working with God to bring in a new kind of society that values people over profit.

Desmond Tutu in his book, *God Has A Dream*, says:

> God calls us to be his partners to work for a new kind of society where people count, where people matter more than things, more than possessions, where human life is not just respected but positively revered, where people will be secure and not suffer from fear of hunger, from ignorance, from disease, where there will be more gentleness, more caring, more sharing, more compassion, more laughter, where there is peace and not war.[1]

One amazing woman the team and I have become friendly with over our trips has seen more than her share of suffering. Elizabeth has lost seven children to preventable diseases such as malaria and diarrhoea. We got chatting one time and ever since, every time we've been to Ghana, we've been to see Elizabeth. On one visit she told us one of her surviving daughters,

---

[1] Desmond Tutu, *God Has A Dream* (Rider & Co, 2005).

Shanice, was in hospital and asked if we would go and see her to pray for her. The whole team piled into the minibus and off we went, but when we arrived we quickly realised the hospital conditions were even worse than we had expected. The heat was suffocating; there were flies everywhere and there weren't even sheets on the mattresses. She was crowded into a room with six other people including a baby who cried the whole time, stopping any of the other patients from getting any sleep. Michelle, one of our team who was also a trained nurse, was disgusted with the conditions and said she wouldn't even want to take a cat in there to be treated let alone human beings.

Shanice was just 18 months old, the same age as my son, Daniel, who was back home with Diane and my daughter, Keziah. She was hooked up to a drip, and when we asked what the mark was on the fluids bag, they said that once the fluid got to that point, Shanice's money had run out and she would be sent home. We were horrified because we knew that without this she could die pretty quickly. We asked how much further treatment would cost and it was just a few pounds. The team quickly dug around to see what cash we could scrape up between us, and thankfully found enough for her to continue her treatment. It shocked us to the core to think that she would have been dead for want of a small amount of money and Elizabeth would have to bury her eighth child.

Not all the hospitals were as bad; in Agogo they were trialling a new drug to treat malaria (which is the cause of over 3,000 deaths a year in Ghana). We spent some time there on the children's ward and met some fantastic kids whose courage and joy was a challenge and an inspiration. One beautiful girl looked like her leg had been badly burnt but the nurse told us it was a skin disease caused by extreme poverty. You wouldn't have known the pain she was in by the huge smile on her face. She and many of the other kids loved the puppet shows we did and the songs we sang; they were just so excited to have people showing them attention and giving them something other than their pain to think about. Some of them were a bit overwhelmed and actually cried as they'd never seen a white person before and were quite shocked by our appearance.

There were many times when we were overwhelmed by the things we saw, and we had to cling to the fact that we were just trying to worship God through our actions. One day we were literally surrounded by hundreds of people as soon as we arrived in a village, some wanting to touch us, some wanting money, others needing prayer and it was just too much; we didn't know what to do. People were pushing us from every direction. We felt completely helpless and hopeless – we didn't have enough to help everyone so we stopped and just started singing 'Here I Am to Worship' to help us fix our eyes on God and to remind ourselves that this was part of our adoration of him. Our motives had to be about having God's heart as that was the only thing that would carry us through, help us to give when we felt like we had nothing left and help us to trust when we wanted to do so much more than we were able to. The atmosphere in the village totally changed and we spent hours praying with people.

Recently we returned to Danpong, the village where the secondary school is being built, and met someone we'd not seen before: Mary. She invited Michelle and me into her home and told us she'd had loads of children who had children of their own but they'd all left to go to the city to find work. She had just one daughter still at home. We asked where her husband was and she said he'd taken a bad fall about 18 months ago and cut his foot and had been in bed ever since. Michelle explained she was a trained nurse and asked if she could see him, so Mary invited us in. Her husband's foot was bandaged with a sock and Michelle, being a far braver person than I, peeled it off to find he'd lost three of his toes and his flesh was literally wasting away. It would have cost him just £1 to have been treated at the hospital but apart from not having the money he couldn't actually get himself to the hospital which was at least an hour's walk away. We had a look at what medical supplies we could find among the team and Michelle managed to bandage him up in a more hygienic way, and then we headed back to the house we were staying in.

I'd no sooner set foot inside the house when I felt in my heart we just had to go back and tell him that Jesus loved him. We didn't know how long he would live so as I shared with the team they all caught the sense of urgency. This old man was so ill he didn't appear to be of much value to the people around him because he couldn't do anything. It felt like people were just waiting for him to die because they knew, at the funeral when everyone would come back from the big cities, there would be a massive party with a lot of alcohol.

When we arrived back at his house he couldn't get his head around it. The first time he saw us he put it down to fluke that we had arrived in his remote village and had been able to help him; the second time he was really confused. We told him we'd contacted the hospital and that they would be coming to pick him up to take him to hospital to diagnose what was going on and to treat him. He kept saying he was nothing, worth nothing, couldn't walk and was no use to anyone, but we told him about Jesus and asked if we could pray. A huge tear rolled down his cheek as he said yes.

At the same time, the team who had stayed in London were texting us to let us know there had been some fatal stabbings and shootings of teenagers in Peckham. Part of me wished I was back home, able to be present in a community that was trying to make sense of such horrendous death and violence. Knowing us for our work in schools with teenagers, the media were asking for interviews with members of the XLP team, and it was hard not to feel that we should have been at home. But the reality was that Peckham could carry on without me and XLP had plenty of staff who were there to help out. God had sent us to a tiny, remote village in Ghana, to minister to one man who no one else seemed to care about. That's the kingdom of God, because people don't have to be all over the news for God to know about them and care about them. If we're willing, he will send us to some bizarre places to let individuals and communities know that he cares for and loves them, and not just from afar.

When we did return to London, the Ghanaians we knew loved the fact that I had been to their country, though some of the kids took some convincing to believe me. The lessons I learned about slavery helped me understand a little bit about black history, as I had never been taught anything about slavery at school. I learned a lot about cultural sensitivities and how important the role of the family unit is and how within that there are many different roles that family members play. I also came to realise that many of the problems we have in this country come from stereotyping people of different cultures from our own and believing everything the media feeds us.

Chatting to some of the black majority church leaders was very helpful as was hearing stories of black people arriving in England after World War 2. Having been invited to come here by the British government it was something of a nasty shock to receive (in many cases) a hostile welcome. This led to some black churches being formed so people could come together and worship with others in the same position.

I also realised that in our evangelism we have portrayed a Eurocentric Jesus: a white guy with blond hair wearing a nightdress and not the Jesus of the Bible. There are many pictures of the Last Supper in which the disciples and Jesus are white and Judas' skin colour is a shade or two darker. The same group can also appear where everyone is black. The challenge to us as the church today is to work cross-culturally as we live in a multi-cultural society with very diverse schools and communities. As Les, in his excellent book, *Relevant Church*, points out:

> A multi-cultural church is one which incorporates diversity and equality at all levels: a church where the reality of people's lives is expressed and appreciated, where people are encouraged to teach others about their cultures and where Christians are developed and pastored in the context of their cultural background. It is a place where different races and cultures help to form the policies and the vision and through them the Complexion of the church is shaped.[2]

The only meaningful way of reaching out to people from different cultures is to get in relationship with them, to make friends, to hang out and to be in a place where we can learn from each other.

---

[2] Les Isaac, *Relevant Church* (Ascension Trust).

9

Preaching Up a Storm

Many of the people in south east London have a Caribbean heritage, so Les suggested I join him and a few friends on a trip to St Vincent to understand the culture issues there. It was the first time I had been to the Caribbean and I found that St Vincent is a picturesque island with white coral sand beaches, clear waters and palm trees.

We were staying in a house high up on the island with a wonderful view looking out over the bay. When we arrived, as we sat on the balcony watching the boats coming into the harbour, Les told me that almost everyone on the island had come there through slavery. He said many wished they could return to Africa, but the country was not the same place their relatives had left behind. Sitting in such beauty it was a sobering reminder of the reason for our trip and brought to mind again a friend of mine who had tried without success to trace her family history. Her grandfather had been a slave – meaning he took on his owner's name and his own family name was lost for ever. The issues of identity and history are complex, especially for those who have been robbed of knowing where they have come from.

The person we were staying with on the island was Pastor Robinson, a very traditional minister who was well-known by everyone on the island. When the next day a few of us wanted to head out alone he just said, 'If anyone gives you any hassle, then tell them you're with me.' There is such a sense of respect for pastors that just being known by Pastor Robinson was our pass to safety. It amazed me that he seemed to have so much authority; whatever he asked someone to do, they would do it. On our first day there Les needed a haircut and, as we were driving along, Pastor Robinson called over to a young guy and asked him to take Les to a barber and to make sure he was OK. Sure enough the lad dropped what he was doing and did exactly what he was told; such is the respect for their elders.

The churches were quite formal and Les told me in no uncertain terms that I needed to smarten up before I could set foot inside one. I've never dressed up for church in my life but on St Vincent they wear their very best, knowing that they are worshipping the King of kings. Les put it bluntly, 'You can't tell people about Jesus in shorts.'

When I'd found an appropriate pair of trousers I spoke at the Revival Centre about the issues that affect young people. Les had told me it was OK to talk about identity and sexuality as he was keen to bring some more openness into the churches which never usually addressed these issues. The congregation were slightly apprehensive but open because Les had told them he was OK with what I was about to speak on. It was amazing the freedom such a simple thing brought for the young people as they began to talk about what troubled them. So much so that we immediately started planning to return the following year and hold a youth conference where we could spend some more time with the young people.

Each night we did an open-air mission and on the first night I got heckled. A group of Rastas who were all high started shouting, 'White boy! White boy!' I was literally the only white man there so it was pretty obvious they were shouting at me. 'You ain't tellin' me nothing,' they said, looking quite put out that I was even there. Sometimes if someone gives me grief while I'm preaching I stop and banter with them, but here I felt completely out of my depth. I didn't have any choice but to carry on preaching as best I could. But they had really rattled me.

As I went back to Pastor Robinson's house the words kept ringing in my ears and I doubted why I was there. I spoke to Les and told him I didn't know what I was doing or even why I was doing it. What if no one could relate to me? Who did I think I was to be able to come to somewhere so different and think I had something of value to say? I'd come here because I wanted to cross the cultural boundaries I'd come across in London, but was totally disheartened. Les said in his own blunt way, 'You need to stop apologising for being white – that's just who you are. God himself has called you to come here and you don't come as a white person, you come as a man of God. You can't be intimidated by skin colour – we're all the same in the kingdom of God.'

It was hard for me to believe but I went out the next night trying to stand firm in my identity in God. When the same guys started having a go again I said as firmly as I could, 'I don't come as someone from England, I come as a man of God. If you listen to what I have to say, it might just change your life.' I was sweating thinking they might get angry and make even more noise in heckling me but it just shut them up. Les added, 'This man is trying to change the world, what are you doing?' And suddenly they started paying attention.

It might sound as if I have a lot of confidence but like anyone I do get scared and nervous about the things that God calls me to. I often worry about being misunderstood and people thinking 'Who does he think he is?' when I try and communicate something I'm passionate about. I also have a bad habit of comparing myself, unfavourably, with every other speaker I've heard. There's always someone more articulate, more intelligent, someone who has more faith than me or who is funnier. Every time I think things can't get more bizarre or scary then they do, like on our third night in St Vincent.

It was the second of a series of three open-air meetings and though Jimmy (a leader of a church in London who we had travelled with) was the speaker, Les and I were expected to sit on the stage all suited up. Although Jimmy's a fairly quiet guy, when he gets a microphone in his hand he completely changes. There were about 300 people gathered from the local community, some Christians and some not, and after an extended time of worship, Jimmy went for it. As he started talking, great splodges of rain began to fall. In the Caribbean you don't have much time between the first spots and a torrential downpour so everyone started running for cover under the nearby school roof. An almighty shout came over the loudspeaker: 'STOP!' Everyone turned to look and it was Jimmy standing stock-still on the stage. 'Do you want to see a miracle?' he asked. There was a resounding yes from the gathered group and we all watched in amazement as he looked to heaven and said, 'In the name of God I command the rain to stop!' We were even more amazed when the rain did just that!

At the same time as I was getting excited at just having seen such an awesome answer to prayer, I had a funny feeling in my stomach. 'Pity the guy who has to stand up tomorrow night and follow that,' I thought. Then the realisation hit me that the poor guy was me! I spent the rest of the evening begging God not to let it rain the following evening. 'I'm sorry for my recent sins, just please don't let it rain,' I said. 'I'm sorry for the sins of the past, everything I've ever done wrong since I was born, just please don't let it rain.' I was even confessing the sins of my ancestors and the entire world, just begging God not to let a raindrop fall. My stomach wasn't quite right for the next 24 hours and though I said I'd eaten something dodgy, I knew it was nerves.

All day I watched the sky like a hawk, every cloud causing me to repent of another sin and to beg for God's mercy, every ray of sunshine a reason to praise. As we headed to the school for the evening's meeting the stormy clouds above were nothing compared to those in my head. It remained dry as we worshipped but I wasn't planning on taking any chances and decided I'd preach my shortest ever sermon in the hopes of it staying dry. No sooner had Pastor Robinson introduced me and I was alone in front of the crowd, than I felt a raindrop on my hand. 'You have to be kidding me,' I thought desperately. But sure enough it was followed by another and another until I couldn't deny any longer that it was starting to rain. No one budged this time; they all just turned to me and waited. They'd seen Jimmy do it and now apparently it was my turn.

All my insecurities flooded to the surface; I had never been more aware of how inadequate I was. In this moment when I felt I had nothing, I came back to the place of remembering that it wasn't about me or my reputation and in my head I said to God, 'I'm not the world's best preacher but you have called me here to bless these people. I've been worried about how I will look if it rains; what people will think of me; but the truth is, this is about blessing them because they've travelled all this way to be here and to hear about you. God, I know you can use me despite my inadequacies because your word says that your power is made perfect in my weakness. I am your child.'

I took a deep breath, shut my eyes so I wouldn't have to see the expectant faces in front of me and said, with as much authority as I could muster (which really wasn't very much), 'God please stop the rain.' My eyes stayed shut for a few more minutes before I realised I couldn't feel any more drops; the rain had stopped! It had worked! The tiny murmured prayer of a sinner like me with so little faith had been heard by God Almighty and he'd stopped the rain when I asked him to. After that my faith shot through the roof and I preached with all my heart.

With families on St Vincent's often being so fragmented, at the end we said we'd like to pray for anyone who was facing troubles in their family and needed God's help. Loads of people came forward and the four of us on the team prayed for all of them. As we finished praying for the last person, the heavens opened and the rain came down! We had to leg it before we got completely soaked, but we had pretty big grins on our faces as we did; God had made his point that he had kept the evening dry for us so people could hear his word and meet with him.

The following year we headed back to St Vincent for the youth conference we had planned on our first trip. Les wasn't able to come but suggested that before we went to St Vincent we should visit Guyana to find out more about their cultural issues. By the time we went to Guyana I thought I was quite prepared for our visit, having been on a number of mission trips by then, but I soon realised it was like nowhere I'd ever been before.

Guyana is one of the poorest countries in South America and has a high proportion of street children and crime. There are ever-increasing reports of kidnappings, car-jackings, home invasions and robberies. The murder rate is three times that of the United States. The country is completely divided between the black and Indian communities with quite a lot of tension between the two.

Just a few months before we arrived, inmates from Georgetown Prison had escaped and caused a huge security scare. Five of them had shot and stabbed their way out of the jail, armed with an AK-47, and hijacked a car to make their escape. Since then they had been terrorising local people with a lengthy list of crimes. They routinely hijacked cars to commit violent robberies, and there were regular shootings, beatings and kidnappings, all believed to be connected to these escapees.

As we drove down the street from the airport, there were bullet holes in many of the wooden houses and we were told there had been a gunfight the night before. There were ditches in the road which made driving very difficult; apparently local thieves would dig them to make cars slow down so they could rob them more easily. Several houses had black flags hanging outside and when we asked what they were representing we were told that the Hindus hung them when they had made a human sacrifice. It was enough to make you pretty fearful but my immediate threat seemed to be from the mosquitoes that all seemed to have PhDs. I swear I used every repellent there is and I was still being bitten to shreds. At least it briefly took my mind off the more serious dangers!

The plan for the five days of our visit was to take some school assemblies, visit a children's home and visit a number of different churches. Some of the Christians in Guyana were amazingly inspiring. One church I spoke in at a mid-week event had a sand-pit in the middle of the building as they didn't have enough money to finish building a pulpit. They had the most awful PA system that crackled and fed back and their instruments were limited to dustbin lids as drums. Their lives at home weren't easy with many women left alone to bring up the children while their husbands had disappeared. Some of the women had lost more than one child to drugs and crime. Yet when it was time to worship they let nothing hinder their praise of God.

The first song we sang was 'Jesus, Lover of My Soul' and they really meant it when they sang 'it's all about you, Jesus'. They weren't focusing on the problems that surrounded them or their lack of good things, they just wanted to glorify and honour Jesus for all that he had done in their lives. As they sung their hearts out I was blown away by the sincerity in their worship and challenged to remember to praise like that during the good and hard times in my life.

On our first Sunday our host, Desmond, took us to the church where I was preaching and marched me to sit in the front row. The pastor stood up and welcomed us and then the worship began. Jimmy was happy behind his video camera, recording everything to show everyone back home. When the worship ended we stood up and introduced ourselves and I started preaching. Suddenly, Desmond started making faces at me and I couldn't quite tell what he meant but he looked worried. I'm notorious for saying the wrong word (like the time I told a group of leaders that the most important thing they needed to remember, the only thing that would bring the change they were looking for was . . . dramatic pause . . . pears! What I had meant to say was 'prayer' but I'd sat down before I realised my blunder.) So anyway, here in Guyana I wondered what mistake I had made this time. Eventually Desmond sidled up to me and told me to wrap things up pretty quickly as he'd realised we were in the wrong church! We'd totally invaded someone else's service and they hadn't even stopped me from preaching. 'Embarrassing' doesn't quite cover it.

I'd only just forgiven Desmond for that humiliation when he landed another bombshell on me. With a big smile on his face he said, 'I've arranged for you to speak at Georgetown Prison tomorrow.' I tried to return his grin, pretending I was pleased and therefore tougher than I actually was but all I could think about was every awful fact we'd heard about the prison since we'd arrived. Georgetown was originally built for 100 prisoners but now had 900 inmates crammed in who had been found guilty of things like murder, robbery and drug smuggling.

That night I was terrified and prayed extremely hard, focusing on every bit of spiritual warfare I could remember. Funny how fear can concentrate your prayers.

The building was pretty ominous; it looked very old-fashioned, like something I had only seen at the movies. The security checks did nothing to reassure me. To get to the chapel we had to walk through a courtyard and past all the men who stood at the bars of their cells, intimidating me with their stares. Sister Faye was the chaplain, a black American woman who had dreamt about the prison and felt God calling her to go and work there. She'd even seen some individual inmates' faces in her dreams and she carried the real authority of someone who knows that God has called them to a specific place.

The chapel was tiny but almost 300 of the toughest looking men I have ever seen were crammed in. Sister Faye introduced me and as I got up I noticed the guards all heading for the doors. My stomach lurched. 'Not now!' I wanted to shout, 'Come back and make me feel safe,' but it was one of those moments when you think, 'Either I believe God has called me here and will protect me or I'm in trouble.' Amazingly, everyone listened quietly while I spoke about Jesus being the friend of sinners. I talked about how he chose to hang around with people whose lives weren't turning out in the way they thought they would. I didn't know what to expect in terms of a response but I have never seen such a genuine and powerful move of the Holy Spirit in a meeting. Almost 90 per cent of the men came forward wanting to be prayed for either for healing or to become Christians. It was such a privilege to see these hardened men humble themselves before God and it reminded me that what heaven desires and hell fears is that we step out of our comfort zones. I hadn't wanted to be there but God had wanted to meet with all those men and tell them that whatever they had done, he still loved them.

It felt like I learned a lot from the prisoners, too, in terms of vulnerability. It's so important that we stay tender so we trust in God and not ourselves and remain intimate with him but it often doesn't seem like a 'manly' thing to do. We're not always very good at showing our feelings, often blaming the British 'stiff upper lip' mentality, but Jesus showed us that it was good to be vulnerable by crying in front of his disciples. The prisoners didn't want theological debates and clever answers, they wanted to be understood. We can often complicate what needs to be done when all people want is for someone to come to them and see their pain caused by the circumstances that have led to their life being that way.

10

All That You Can Be

With so many diverse cultures at the different London schools we were working in, we began to look for an activity that wouldn't favour one ethnic group over another and would unite them in a common goal. For it to work it had to be a level playing field so language skills and cultural background couldn't be allowed to hinder the pupils. Previously, an *ad hoc* talent show had been run at one of the schools and had gone down very well, sparking the idea that we could make this a much bigger and better event. The arts are a great way for young people to express themselves, and we were excited to see if many of the kids who didn't do well academically would here have an opportunity to excel. The first show we ran in a school was in the gym of the Kingsdale School in Peckham and we were completely amazed at the talent we discovered there.

The hit of the show was Tiffany, who was on the verge of being excluded. She was a very cute but seriously badly behaved girl with a major issue with authority and a real attitude. No one knew quite what to expect when she took to the stage, but when she started to sing the whole of the previously rowdy room just shut up. In a stunningly clear voice she sang Mariah Carey's 'Hero' about finding faith in yourself; she blew everyone away. Even with the terrible acoustics of the building she sounded amazing. She rightfully took first place and everyone was surprised that this girl who was known for behaving so badly was the success story of the evening.

As a team we were so encouraged. All the young people loved it, with both those taking part and those watching saying they wanted to do it all again. Even the ones who didn't win enjoyed the whole experience and felt that they had achieved something just by getting up and performing. The teachers were gobsmacked at the talent in the school and the parents were given reasons to be proud of their children.

I was so excited about the reaction to the talent show that my mind started to work overtime. 'How about doing one of these in every school we work in?' I said to the team enthusiastically. 'We could then take the winners from each school and do a borough final. It would be amazing; we could hire a theatre for the final and get local newspapers down. It would be a fantastic way of bringing not only schools and families together but whole communities.'

Some of the team were keen but lots of them told me it was a daft idea and would never happen. 'There's too much gang rivalry between the schools; if you get them in the same room competing they'll end up killing each other,' they said. I wasn't put off, in fact it just made me more determined to make it happen and to prove them wrong! So many times we just accept the way things are and let that stand in the way of how they should be. I had hope that we could do something through the arts that could achieve things the rest of our schools work couldn't. We started speaking to the schools we were going into and everyone responded enthusiastically.

For our first borough final we spent weeks doing auditions during lunchtimes and after school. We had to track down equipment we could borrow, as many of the children couldn't afford the things they needed, and we worked hard to make sure all the parents knew about it and were invited. On the night, seeing hundreds of parents and pupils packed into the Civic Centre on the Old Kent Road was a real answer to prayer but it also added a fair amount of pressure. The XLP team and I all stood nervously around the hall wondering if this was about to be a painful few hours or whether somehow the young people could pull it off.

David was one of the first to perform. He was from the Aylesbury Estate and hadn't shown much promise in class, in fact he was constantly being told off for drumming on the desks. This turned to his advantage when we saw that by doing this he had taught himself how to play the congas and was an exceptionally gifted drummer. Everyone was completely amazed, not least the 20 members of his family who had come to watch him. After David received third prize his dad came up to me with tears in his eyes. He had no idea his son had such talent and was more used to getting phone calls from teachers to say David was in detention again than he was to hearing people praise his son. For the first time, David's dad had a real sense of pride in his son and was overwhelmed by seeing him perform in front of hundreds of people.

Earlier we'd received a phone call to say that Mona, a beautiful Year 8 Nigerian girl, wasn't able to make it. Mona had been rejected and abandoned by her parents who had moved back to their home in Nigeria, leaving her with an aunt, and at the last minute the aunt had said she wouldn't give Mona a lift to the show. She'd shown such talent that immediately one of the team dropped what they were doing and raced to pick her up so she could take part. She sang beautifully and wowed the judges who awarded her second place, winning her a trip to Premier Radio where she sang live on air. The boost to her self-esteem was incredible. 'My parents told me I wouldn't amount to anything,' she said. 'But now I'm showing them what I can do.'

For a long time at XLP we'd longed to bless not only the pupils but their families as well and here was an opportunity to do just that. The verse, 'God sets the lonely in families',[1] had never seemed more important and we were keen to use this opportunity to help the young people connect with their own families.

The talent show became what we call the 'Arts Showcase' to make it sound less like something you'd find at Butlins and to give the kids some credibility! It's now happening in each of the four boroughs that we work in, culminating with a huge showcase each summer where we usually have around 16 acts with 300 people cheering them on. We've seen loads of different performances, including magicians, Irish dancers, solo singers, bands, rappers, MCs and even had scenes from Shakespearean plays performed. Given the opportunity, many of the young people have really shone in their gifts. For the first time many have had a reason to apply themselves, to practise in order to get better so they could prove to others and to themselves all that they could be. We also try to have

---

[1] Psalm 68:6

inspirational role models as our judges, and over the last few years have had members of the London Community Gospel Choir, DJs, actors from the TV show *The Bill* and up-and-coming music stars like the band, Fierce, who had just come back from touring with Whitney Houston. We try to get musicians and singers in as special guests, too, so that they can perform while the judges make their decision, which helps to make the event an extra special evening.

We encourage everyone now to write their own material and not just to perform covers, and again we've been surprised at the talent this has unearthed. For many of these young people who have a hard time expressing themselves, they can use this opportunity to have their say. Even those who can't speak very good English can take the opportunity to show what they can do as they can pick whatever act they like, breaking down more cultural and language barriers. For those who want to, we interview them during the evening, asking them questions about what their goals and ambitions are and what issues they struggle with. Again it's a great opportunity for them to say how they feel but it also gives a chance for peer-on-peer education, something the kids really listen to and respect.

All this means that the Arts Showcase has developed into not only a show but a platform for young people to have a voice about what is happening in their lives and their community. At the most recent show, young people had a lot to say about recent shootings in the area. One young person said, 'I am sick of hearing about black-on-black crime, how come you never hear about white-on white crime?' Others talked about the lack of opportunities to get decent jobs.

For us it's another lesson in listening. A lot has been said about the issues facing young people in inner cities but what we really need to do is listen to them. I fear sometimes the government and others are coming up with policies and legislation without even consulting the people who are in the thick of the action and have something to say. Many young people feel that the areas they live in are always being viewed in a negative light, particularly when TV documentaries about South East London focus on all the worst issues. While no one is pretending those issues are not there, the Arts Showcase gives young people the opportunity to show everyone that people living in South East London are also extremely talented and have something to say about the world around them.

Those taking part inevitably invite loads of friends and family to come and cheer them on in the heats and in the final. This means the audiences are usually made up of around 99 per cent non-churchgoers. It's another way that we can reach out to people, rather than inviting them to a church service that is a million miles from their lives. It's the first step to showing that we're interested in young people's lives and just want them to excel in all they do. For those who are suspicious of Christianity it just helps to break down another barrier.

We've been amazed at how it has helped kids from different schools to work together too. Although they are competing against one another there is an overriding feeling that they are all doing something together – they have to want each other to do well so that the whole evening is a success. We've even seen rival schools gathering together to pray before an event; something no one ever thought would happen on so many levels!

There have been some tensions as well, like at a recent

showcase final where a lad from Peckham was performing. He is part of a notorious gang, known and hated by another gang from Lewisham. There's massive rivalry between the Peckham and Lewisham postcodes; if you come from one and walk into the other with your gang you're basically asking for a fight. If you walk in alone you're asking for trouble. Thankfully we got wind of the fact that the Lewisham boys were going to rush the event to cause trouble so we made sure we had extra people on the door and were grateful they didn't arrive until after Jordan had performed. When we saw they were close by we whisked him out of the back door and breathed a sigh of relief when the gang turned and left, realising they wouldn't get what they came for.

It was a risk bringing together rival schools but the events have really helped calm things down between them on many occasions and it's been a real breakthrough to see rival schools working together over an evening to produce a good show, or cheering for one another rather than fighting.

At one event on the Old Kent Road all the major gangs in the South East were there. This road divides the borough in two and gang culture is so strong that many won't cross the street from their side and kids from the schools are virtually at war with one another. We were a little wary of trouble but the atmosphere was absolutely amazing and we had one of the best showcases we've ever had. The hall was totally packed with all the schools and gangs and yet there wasn't a single problem inside. In fact our main problem was that too many people turned up so we had to turn away loads of very disappointed young people.

We now have an Arts Co-ordinator, Leo, who works full time organising the shows and with the young people to help them develop their talents. We are passionate about people achieving all that they can and we know there is a responsibility to take the talent we've seen and give the kids every opportunity to do well in that area. We're working on building a studio in our offices where they can record demos, something they would never otherwise have the opportunity to do, and we will do everything we can to open doors for them in other areas, too.

Some of the young people have used the Arts Showcase as a platform to other things – such as one boy band from a school in Lewisham who went on to perform at the Queen's Golden Jubilee celebrations in Hyde Park. The showcase is such a simple idea but it achieves so much for so many kids and demonstrates to them, to their schools and to their families just how much they have to contribute to our communities.

Below are some lyrics from Amenah who has entered the Arts Showcase four times and went on to win the Lewisham showcase final. We have seen a real change in her, and the lyrics to this song she performed describe what has been going on in her life.

> I remember you told me I couldn't make it
> You doubted me undoubtedly made me so sad
> You thought that I couldn't take it
> You told me that I would be nothing, without you
> Look at me now.

Here I am, I got my swagger back, you just can't hold me down
So sing along to my brand new song
Here I am, have my spirits high, your lies have got no hold
So kick back and watch me fly.

Now my mother used to say to me that some don't have eyes to see
The beauty that's inside of me, but they will see eventually.
Now I've witnessed it with my own eyes
The growth of what I had inside
Humbleness took over pride
That's when I knew I had arrived.

See I've been doing my own thing
You should be doing yours
So why you wanna hate on me?
No matter what I do it's never enough
I never hurt no one so tell me
Why you wanna hate on me?[2]

---

[2] Reproduced by permission.

11

XL R8

XLP was growing fast; we now had 60 lunch clubs a month and were working in over 30 schools, with demand for more, yet it still felt like we were missing something.

In the London boroughs we work in crime is generally well above the national average and the most likely time for crimes to be committed is between 4 pm and 6 pm. This is the classic time that kids are out of school, looking for something to do, and the majority of their parents are out working so unable to supervise them. It was all very well for us to go into schools and talk to the young people about making good choices, but we knew we also needed to provide a practical response to help them stay away from crime. The answer we dreamt of was a bus that we could take onto the estates the kids lived in, providing things for them to do, ways for us to help them with their homework and to give us a further chance to get to know them and support them. We had a vision to convert a standard double-decker bus into a moving youth centre that would have room for both educational and leisure activities. We wanted to have everything, from laptops so we could help kids with their homework, to a space where there would be board games and Play Stations.

Charlotte, one of our previous gap-year students who had become the Southwark borough leader, had a particular passion to do more on the Aylesbury Estate. It is an area best known as one of the biggest estates in Europe; 98 per cent of it council housing in the form of huge grey tower blocks. It hasn't got a very good reputation, with drink and drug problems, and much lower A–C grade GCSE passes than the rest of the borough (which is itself lower than most in the country). We found out some crazy statistics that in a community survey in 2002, only 29 per cent of residents felt safe walking alone in the area after dark compared to a national average of 66 per cent. The rate of crime for the Aylesbury Estate area is 408 crimes per 1,000 of the population compared to 171 crimes per 1,000 for Southwark.

We didn't want to be put off by the way people viewed the Aylesbury Estate but had a vision to bring some light to the 7,500 people living there, including the 2,000 young people. We started by approaching local residents about the needs of young people and found out they were really keen for us to provide something directly after school. Although there was youth work happening on the estate, many of the young people weren't engaged in the activities and residents felt they needed something else. As Charlotte met with different people on the council and local community groups she found that the residents' enthusiasm wasn't matched by these people who barely wanted to give her the time of day. Something in her heart told her that God was in this and she wasn't put off. Week after week she slogged at it, getting meetings with as many people as she could and undertaking a community audit by knocking on doors on the estate. She spoke to as many residents as she could, getting facts and figures to take to the council and to inform our planning to make sure the bus would provide the services most needed.

Eventually there was an answer to prayer: during Soul in the City in 2004 (a mission to London organised by Soul Survivor) we made contact with a youth worker on the estate who said that if we could get a bus he'd be really happy for us to park it outside his youth centre. Of course we had no money for a bus but in another amazing breakthrough Southwark Council said they would lend us theirs. They needed it for promotions four times a year but the rest of the time it was ours and they even fitted it out to our specifications, the only drawback being that they had it painted bright pink! Despite it being a bit embarrassing it actually had its advantages as everyone could see us coming and people started talking about the big pink double-decker bus that kept turning up on the estate.

We wrote to all the parents that we had previously visited on the estate telling them what we were doing and inviting them to come and have a look if they wanted and to send their children. The youth drop-in sessions were a huge success. We were approached by a local school to do some homework support with a group of students who needed a bit of extra help. The school would identify a group that needed help, we would write to them and then go on home visits and keep a record of progress which would be reviewed by their teacher.

This turned out to be a good thing in the case of Shanique. When we asked Shanique's mum if she had received our letter she looked vague but said she recognised the XLP logo. We told her about the homework club we were running and asked if she would like her daughter to attend. She responded enthusiastically and explained that she herself couldn't read or write, but felt that if we could teach Shanique, then perhaps Shanique could teach her. It was heartbreaking to hear her describe her frustration at not being able to help her daughter with her homework and her studies. Shanique became one of our regular homework club attendees and planted the idea in us that some day we'd like to be able to help not only the young people but their parents as well.

One of the schools asked us to work with a twelve-year-old boy called Junior who needed some extra help with his homework. He was a very sweet kid but had quite serious problems with dyslexia which had held him back. He was on a reduced school timetable as he found the social and academic demands of a full schedule too demanding.

We went to his house and spoke to him and his mum about our club on the bus and how we were planning an eight-week homework club we hoped he'd be a part of. Initially his mum was suspicious about what we were doing and was worried Junior would be picked on by older children as he struggled to make friends. When she found out that one of the guys on our team had dyslexia she relaxed a bit and decided to let him come. Over the weeks we realised that Junior was amazing at maths so we always made sure we finished with that so he left on a high. He gradually formed friendships with the other kids in the club and got to know some of the XLP team, his confidence and self-esteem growing with every session. He felt able to attend school more regularly and his standard of work began to improve too. Each week his mum would come to collect him and have a chat about how he was getting on. At one of the last sessions she thanked Charlotte who'd been working closely with Junior and said she was so grateful we were willing to work with her son. She'd seen his confidence boosted in just a couple of months and he was so much happier as a result.

That's one of the great advantages of the bus – rather than inviting people to come to us, we can go to them and be a part of their everyday lives. Much of the evangelism in this country is about trying to persuade people to come to our meetings or events, but Jesus' last instruction to us was to *go*.

We have been taking the bus onto the Aylesbury Estate every week for almost three years now and it is one of the weekly highlights for many of the team. There are about 200 kids from the estate on our register and every week we get between 20 and 50 coming along. It is an easy place for them to come and chill out, relax and have fun with their mates, but also a place where they know there are adults to talk to and who will listen to them. Many of them have been coming from the beginning and it is great to see them growing up. It is a privilege to be part of the work, and even though it is tough (as youth work is at times) it is also very exciting to be around. The estate and the people on it might have been written off by society and only known for all the bad statistics, but there is a lot more to it than that. These young people have so much to offer; they are interesting, inspirational and once you get under the sometimes hard exterior you will find some wonderful young people who at the end of the day are just looking for a little bit of love, respect and affirmation.

We soon found that by using the bus we were able to reach a far wider age group than we were in the schools. Many of the families on the estate consider the whole estate their home, so it's not unusual to see very young children wandering around, seemingly unsupervised. One of our eXperience students, Kerry, always talks about a three-year-old boy, Imarni, who brings himself along to the bus each week. He's a really cute kid who already carries an attitude of someone much older, wearing a scarf tied around his face and talking about his 'olders' (the guys who he looks up to on the estate). At such a young age he's used to looking after himself, but when he comes on the bus he gets to be just a little boy again. Often he'll sit on Kerry's lap and play with her earrings, chatting away or letting her read to him.

When we get children this young coming and no one collects them at the end of the session, we take them back to their homes, many times finding that there's no one in. No one is waiting for them; no one knows where they are. Sometimes they have been left with a sibling just a few years older and sometimes they are just completely alone. We have to then knock on doors to see if we can find a friend of the family to look after them until their parents return. It's so hard to see this being the daily reality for children so young and makes you realise quite why they value us spending time with them.

Though many people live on these estates, there is a real sense of loneliness with many people retreating into their own personal worlds, making it hard to get alongside them. Mother Teresa once said, 'The greatest disease in the world is not starvation but loneliness. Loneliness is the feeling of not mattering to anyone even when you are surrounded by people.' In a similar way to the lunch clubs we hope the bus will do something to alleviate this loneliness and give the young people a sense of belonging. Though many of them don't like institutions (often having negative and hostile views of both the police and the church) they do respond to places where they can build friendships and where they feel safe to be themselves.

In each session we have what the kids call 'story time', when we all sit down together and talk about something, like how to be a good friend, or self-esteem. Sometimes simple questions give you the most telling answers, for example, when we ask what they're good at. We're often greeted with a resounding silence and when pushed they'll say things like 'kicking people' because they literally can't think of anything else. Violence is a big issue and the kids often talk about stabbings they've seen in such a matter-of-fact way because they've seen so many in their short lives.

In fact it was through a horrific murder that the bus came to be on the Milford Towers Estate in Lewisham. Rochelle Holmes was only 15 when it is thought she was snatched at knifepoint while trying to phone her boyfriend. She was strangled, and her body was found cut into pieces and left in bin bags on the Milford Towers Estate. At this time the bus was only operating in Southwark and Greenwich, and Tim, our Lewisham borough leader, had been trying to work out where in Lewisham the bus should go. The murder happened in the middle of this process, and the local press was full of put-downs and negativity about this tiny estate. They said it was riddled with crack dealers, it wasn't safe, and it was the worst place to live.

It was clear that this was an estate that needed some positive input, and to Tim the bus was the obvious answer. Having not been to the estate before, he went to look around, meet some locals and find out what could be done to help. The estate is a strange mid-twentieth-century design disaster, built above Catford Shopping Centre and going from the third floor up to the seventh. That means you can't get a car up to the estate; you can only go on foot. It's not huge, in fact there are about 280 one- or two-bedroom flats, and the only community centre is a small converted flat in the middle of the estate run by the tenants association and housing association. Tim chatted to Huw and Lisa, who ran the centre, and both were keen on the idea, offering all the assistance they could. 'If you'll bring your bus onto our estate we will personally introduce you to every young person here,' they promised.

The local police were also keen and supportive so Tim and the team were introduced to all the parents, so they could put together a picture of what needed to be done. It was fantastic to chat to the families, being invited into homes, having cups of tea and getting to know what the estate was like, and also interesting trying to communicate to people who spoke little English. The flats, though small, were homely; house-proud parents doing the best they could with the resources they had. Some of the houses were beautiful and being so high up had stunning views of London. It became obvious that there were very few teenagers on the estate, but loads of kids under eleven. Parents resoundingly said they needed after-school activities for their kids, and so this is what we did.

But first we had to work out where you put a bus when you can only get up to an estate by stairs! Between the estate and the shopping centre below there is a floor for delivery trucks and industrial bins. This was the only spot we could use. Even so, it has been a fantastic blessing, allowing us to meet families from the estate, cleaners and shop owners too.

Understandably, the community on the estate had been devastated by Rochelle's murder, a lot of them filing to move house. For the weeks that followed there was an eerie silence on the estate: no children playing, no doors open. It's taken a while but, months on, the community has started to open up again. The bus soon picked up momentum, though we had to walk the kids to and from the estate; some still scared due to the murder. Recently there has been another murder, prompting calls from the media for the estate to be ripped down, negativity dripping from every word. I am convinced, though, that what the children and young people need on estates like Aylesbury and Milford Towers is people who are willing to be there week in and week out. The answer isn't tearing down the estates and displacing communities; we need sustainable youth work projects and not just hit and runs. As the church, our calling is to get involved in the mess of people's lives, offering grace, compassion and a way out of some very difficult circumstances.

We now go onto a different estate on every weekday of the school terms, and on two nights go to two areas to reach more people. When young people see the bus coming from their bedroom window, they run down to see us and we know they value what we're doing. Around 200 children come every week, mainly aged between 6 and 18, and the bus provides much more than just a place to keep them off the streets and out of trouble as we work closely with their schools to provide the best educational support tailored for each group's needs. Demand is growing and more and more schools and estates have asked us to come and work with their young people. Our hope for the future is to have a number of buses so that we can reach more young people in this simple way.

12

Redemption Song

Nothing has done more to highlight the growing problem of violent gangs in South East London than the tragic death of ten-year-old Damilola Taylor. Nigerian-born Damilola had only been in the country for a few months (where his family were seeking help for his sister's epilepsy) when he fell victim to two bullying brothers on his way home from school. It's believed they stabbed him with a broken beer bottle and left him to bleed to death.

The story was reported everywhere, illustrated with Damilola's innocent face smiling out of his school photograph, a moving image highlighting the tragic waste of this young boy's life. It was by no means the only incident in the area but certainly highlighted an increase in gang violence, particularly the common use of guns and knives.

Over the following years things seemed to get worse. I remember calling Diane one night while I was away at Spring Harvest and I could hear police sirens in the background. Although it was very late in the evening our daughter, Keziah, was up, woken by the sounds of gunshots just down the road from our house. It was so frightening knowing that violent crime was happening on our doorstep and I felt powerless to protect my own family.

The statistics did nothing to reassure me: a MORI survey for the Youth Justice Board found that 29 per cent of 11- to 16-year-olds admitted carrying a knife. Research by the Bridge House Trust found there were few specific projects dealing with the issue, and that there was controversy and uncertainty about how best to handle it. It used to be that school teachers confiscated packets of chewing gum; here in one after-school club in Woolwich we had to take live ammo from an eight-year-old. Some schools even started putting in security measures and personnel to relieve students of potentially lethal weaponry as they entered the school, but this was just treating the symptom. New weapons are easily found to replace those confiscated at school or by the police, and of course taking them away doesn't address the reason young people are carrying them in the first place.

It was timely that while we were trying to work out what to do about this issue in London, Les Isaac had set up a trip for us to go to Trenchtown and Antigua. If the violence was getting bad at home, Trenchtown was on a whole other level. We arrived in June and were told that in the first six months of that year 600 people had been shot. Aside from being the former home of Bob Marley, violence seems to be what Trenchtown is most well-known for. It is a small area within Kingston, the capital city of Jamaica, and got its name from the large open-trenched sewer which runs through the neighbourhood because there wasn't enough money for a proper sewer system. The whole area has always been poor but became dangerous and unstable in the 1970s when the

People's National Party took control, putting the area at war with neighbouring Rema, controlled by the Jamaica Labour Party. Colosseum Drive still separates the two areas though there are now many gangs and groups at war with each other. The majority of residents live in dire ghetto conditions; most flats have bullet holes all over their walls and are in such poor condition that they would be condemned in this country. Drug trafficking and extortion are rife.

Les had linked us up with a woman called Lorna Stanley who heads up Operation Restoration, a fantastic project seeking to serve communities in and around Trenchtown. Lorna is a wonderful lady – she was born in Panama and arrived in Jamaica when she was eight – who is passionate about seeing change and is known as the 'Mother of Trenchtown'. Over the last ten years she has set up many programmes covering after-school clubs, outreach into local communities, a 'Youth Off the Streets' initiative and a spiritual enrichment and counselling project as well as an incentive programme.

It was easy to warm to Lorna, not only for her amazing get up and go but also her fearless attitude. She told us how she was approached by gang members and told that if she gave them money, they would protect her. This was said with a gun pointed at her head. I can't say how I'd have responded . . . I'd probably have been searching around for my wallet pretty quickly. Laura, on the other hand, knocked the gun away and said indignantly, 'Who do you think you are? Jesus? He's the only one who protects me!' When I heard that I figured I would be wise to make Lorna my new best friend for the duration of the trip!

Lorna introduced us to Debbie, a local deputy headteacher who would also be guiding us during our visit. Debbie told us that she'd previously been a 'gun girl' for many years meaning she was the one who looked after all the guns for the men in case there was a police raid. She'd just wanted to be loved and accepted and had got her identity from her role and going out with the toughest of the guys.

Debbie's brother was a preacher. One day he was speaking in the middle of Trenchtown when a van drove past and fired a shot that killed him. He was one of many innocent victims of mistaken identity, notorious in drive-by shootings as the killer doesn't always have time to check they have the right person. It was a sickening jolt for Debbie, realising what she'd become involved in, and as she mourned her brother she got herself clean from taking drugs. She went to Operation Restoration where she found Lorna and her team were willing to help her turn her life around. She took some classes, got connected with the church and went on to become deputy head of a local school. One thing I loved about Debbie was that physically she stayed where she was – she was still in the same flat right in the heart of Trenchtown – and in the midst of all the problems there she was able to take her life in a totally different direction.

As Lorna and Debbie walked us around Trenchtown we began to see some of the problems they were up against as they tried to bring hope to the area. The damaged walls in Bullet Alley testified to how it got its name; teenagers hung around on the streets waiting to see what would kick off; Debbie pointed out twelve-year-old boys carrying guns in their pockets; young girls tried to attract attention in tiny skirts and figure-hugging clothes, or nursed pregnant stomachs despite their young age. I'd been to some tough places before but this beat them all, even Kosovo. Yet again I stood out like a sore thumb – the only white man to be seen – and it was incredibly intimidating to be stared at everywhere we went. The air was thick with tension, everyone eyed everyone else suspiciously. Lorna told us the gangs would sleep in shifts with someone always on watch to guard against ambush attacks from rivals. Revenge killings were commonplace but all that did was perpetuate a vicious circle of death and hatred.

Walking past one flat, Lorna told us that a gunman had gone into this house and killed 3-year-old twins as well as a 15-year-old girl who was 38 weeks pregnant. The reason they got shot was that one part of the community had won an election and, while they were celebrating, the other side went into the community and shot the kids.

The community that the 15-year-old belonged to wanted revenge and threatened to take five lives for each one that had been taken from them. The girl's mother went on TV and begged them to see that more death wasn't the answer; in her pain she didn't want another parent to suffer the things she had. In respect to the mother's wishes, the gangs listened to her call for grace and didn't take their revenge – a rare event and an example to the whole community.

'How would you like to do a rap session?' Lorna asked out of the blue, sending fear running right through me. I looked at her as if she was crazy, thinking, 'I'm a stiff white boy, you're not going to see me rap and if you did it really wouldn't be a good thing!' While I tried to find the right words she interpreted the look on my face and said, 'A rap session is where we get together two lots of gangs who are fighting and mediate between them.'

I wasn't sure whether that scared me more or less than having to rap in front of people!

'Do you want to do it?' she asked.

'No, I want to go home,' was my honest response but before I could say it I caught sight of Les's face. 'This is what we came here for,' he said and our fate was sealed.

Operation Restoration had started hiring out school classrooms for these sessions, inviting the groups to drop their weapons and come and talk instead. As we sat waiting for them to come in, my heart was in my mouth and I wondered what I'd got myself into this time. What could I possibly say to these men whose lives had been filled with such pain and violence? But as soon as we started I realised it really wasn't about what I could say but about listening to what they had to say.

One of the guys who had helped to organise the session was a former gang leader called Destruction, and he told me he'd become a hit man, sent on jobs to kill other gang members, until one day he was asked to go and shoot one of his close friends. At that point he knew he couldn't live that kind of lifestyle any more and made a commitment to Christ. He now helps to gather the gangs for sessions like this and works hard to get money to help his young family who are still living in the ghetto. The problems the rest of the gang described sounded depressingly familiar: there was a lack of education in Jamaica, leading to little ambition and hope for the future.

The men described their agony at seeing another generation coming up behind them who couldn't read or write, who had no way of earning enough to look after themselves, with the inevitable result that they would turn to crime. They described the fear that comes with living in a place like Trenchtown where so many people carry a gun and violence is so rife there's a sense that you shoot first or someone shoots you. Once you've shot someone, they said, that's it for life. You can't sleep, you constantly have to watch your back and you're always on the run in case someone takes revenge.

It was fascinating, though heart-wrenching, to find out what was really going on behind the crime statistics, and to see that many of these guys were just struggling to make the best of the limited resources they had, having made some bad choices along the way. It wasn't a time for preaching, it was a time to listen and to understand what life was like for them which they appreciated and respected us for. I told them a bit about what XLP were doing back in England to try and encourage them that there could be change; for them perhaps through organisations like Operation Restoration and Save Jamaica.

We also spoke about believing in yourself, having a healthy self-esteem, and having dignity and respect for life. I'll never forget the looks on their faces when Les said, 'A boy can make someone pregnant, but it takes a man to be a father.' This wasn't a time for easy answers and as we drew to a close Les asked one of our group, Chris, if he would lead us in a song. He chose the Bob Marley classic 'Redemption Song', emphasising the words 'Emancipate yourselves from mental slavery'.

Everyone joined in at that point and I really wished I had known the words as it felt like a powerful heart cry for all the guys in the room.

The next day Lorna had arranged for us to go on a prayer walk with a group of local pastors. In a very poor ghetto area of Rema they stopped outside one particular house and introduced me to the woman who lived there. Her 16-year-old son had been shot dead just the week before, and as I looked into her tear-stained face I knew I had no comprehension of the pain she was going through. Not only was she mourning her son but she was living in fear that her other son would go looking for revenge and potentially lose his own life in the process. Other members of the family gathered so we could pray together and the boy's uncle began to sob uncontrollably as we called out to God. They took us to the place where he had been shot and it brought everything home to me, standing on the very spot where a young lad had lost his life, surrounded by his grief-stricken family.

Our next visit was to a family who said that the previous night they had heard gunshots, and before they knew it gunshots were being fired at their house but they had no idea why. The young mother had grabbed her two small children and hidden under the bed until the firing had stopped.

Towards the end of the prayer walk a police car stopped us and asked us what we were doing, so we explained that we had come to pray for the community. The policeman became very emotional explaining that every time he left his house, his wife and his children, he was scared. His wife would panic every time he was late home in case he had been shot. He said, 'You have no idea how stressful it is doing this job, but I genuinely want to help.' All the pastors who were on the prayer walk and I gathered round the car, held hands and prayed for him, moved by his pain and vulnerability.

My eyes were really being opened to the pain and suffering surrounding this crazy gun crime and violent culture that ruled Trenchtown and my heart ached for the people living in this as their daily reality. The neighbourhood is divided in two by Colosseum Drive and people do not cross from one side to the other. The young people Lorna knew didn't want to live like this and they took us down to the area to see how the roadways are blocked by huge logs, and burnt-out fridges are scattered across the road to try and stop drive-by shootings. Lorna had arranged a two-day open-air event that involved taking a marching band right the way through the no-go areas.

As I walked through the neighbourhood I couldn't help but fear the gang leaders who stood on the street corners, their faces covered by scarves with just their eyes exposed so they could stare at their rival gang members. The expectation was thick in the air that at any moment things could kick off, but I tried not to let it worry me (or at least show that it was worrying me!) until we reached the area where a stage had been set up. After Chris had sung a song, Les gave me a not so gentle nudge and said 'Go on then,' indicating the stage.

I looked at him in horror. 'What do you mean? Why don't you do it?' I asked, trying to keep the begging note out of my voice.

Les shook his head and smiled, saying, 'A lot of white guys don't come to places like this. They're all waiting to hear what you have to say.' It seemed I didn't have much choice, so with my heart in my mouth I made my way up to the platform. I don't think I have ever been so scared in my life, and as I looked up I saw that many faces were hostile, while many more were just completely uninterested. I had to work hard to get their attention and felt that the best thing for me to speak on would be identity.

I told them about a girl we met in one of the Peckham schools. We asked her to give us her thumb print, part of the way we were demonstrating to all the kids that they are unique. Rather than take part like everyone else, she grabbed her coat and bag and ran for the door. 'I'm not special,' she cried, 'I'm nothing.' I talked about how easy it is for us to feel like that when we look at the circumstances of our lives but how God can change anything around. I went on to say that no matter what anyone else thinks of us, God is passionate about us, so passionate about us that he sent his Son to give up his life so that we can know God. It seemed to hit a chord in the crowd.

The biggest challenge for those working in Trenchtown is the emotional state of the young people. More often than not they have had close relatives and friends who have been murdered; their emotions are unstable, their hearts are hard and they don't see any hope of the situation changing. The church is really trying to work with them and is generally really active in the community which was great to see. I visited a banana chip factory where members of the community came to get work – an initiative run by a local church who are keen to provide jobs and education. The same church also runs a home for women who have been thrown out of their homes due to difficult issues within the family. I heard story after story of people saying they felt worthless, neglected and unloved, and now because of the work of Christians in the area they are educated, have jobs and their aim is to be a role model in their community.

Though in many ways Trenchtown has been one of the toughest places I have visited, I left inspired by the people I met and the stories of hope from individuals and can't wait to go back in just a few months. Lorna and her team had no concern for their own personal safety as they have genuine faith that God will look after them. In a recent article for Jamaicans.com Lorna said,

I know the Diaspora feels a sense of hopelessness about what is happening in Jamaica. But, all is not lost. I returned to Jamaica because I believe in the power of one; that according to the Bible, 'One can chase a thousand and two can put ten thousand to flight.' I have seen a significant number of lives being transformed to know that this is true.[2]

---

[2] www.jamaicans.com/articles/primeinterviews/lornastanleyoprestore.shtml

13
Gunz Down

As I returned to Peckham the craziness of Trenchtown wouldn't leave my head. My fear was that if we didn't do something in London we could be looking at things spiralling even further out of control in the same way they had there.

Not long after I returned I received a phone call from Wizdom from hip-hop group GreenJade and it seemed we'd both been struggling with the same issue. The band had been performing at a New Year's Eve party in Birmingham when just a few miles away 17-year-old Letisha Shakespeare and 18-year-old Charlene Ellis were shot dead. You may remember from the news that the gunmen had been aiming at guys who were standing near them who were members of a rival gang, but it was the innocent Letisha and Charlene who lost their lives.

Another night GreenJade were performing in a club in Clapham when a guy came in and pointed a gun at them on stage. He had come looking for someone at the concert. Fortunately no one was hurt in the incident but of course it shook the guys up.

Wiz said they knew they had to do something and had contacted us as they knew we were involved in schools work in areas where gun crime was on the increase. God had brought an answer pretty quickly to the 'What can we do?' question and together with the other members of GreenJade and the XLP team we began planning a tour we could take round schools. The show had to be entertaining and engage the kids but also deliver a strong message. It was fantastic working with GreenJade who are guys that the young people can really look up to and aspire to be like in a really positive way. Not only could they get whole assembly halls going mad while they performed songs like 'Gunz Down' but Wiz could rap about anything with just a few seconds' notice. As part of the show we'd get the kids to bring up on stage anything they could find in their pockets and challenge Wiz to come up with a rap on the spot that featured five of them. Every time, as the objects got more and more bizarre, we'd wonder if he could do it, but each time the kids lapped it up as he did it again. We used drama as well with two of the members of GreenJade acting out a scenario of how something small, like someone owing you some money, can escalate into a bigger situation through small choices.

While I left the rapping, dancing and drama to GreenJade, at each show I'd do a section on making choices. We found out that the three reasons which young people give for carrying weapons is to use them in criminal activity, to have as a fashion accessory and status symbol, or because they are scared of being attacked. The message we were all desperate to get across was that everyone has a choice. As teenagers, in the midst of so much peer pressure and in a culture where violence was becoming the norm, we wanted to make sure they knew that they didn't have to do anything. The emphasis was on not rushing decisions and making life-changing choices in the blink of an eye; not being pushed into decisions because of what anyone else says or does; and lastly, being sussed, i.e. thinking through the consequences of each choice.

Although the tour is called Gunz Down and the emphasis is on guns, the same judgements and decision-making processes are relevant to whether young people carry knives, use their fists to make a point and all kinds of life choices, so we knew it would have a broad appeal. The truth is that much of the violence erupts over nothing; someone treads on someone else's trainer and suddenly there's a gang war and a body count.

Again in many ways I knew the kids were looking at me and thinking, 'What do you know about my life?' but as soon as I started talking about my experiences in Trenchtown they looked at me with a whole new level of respect. A lot of these kids who were pretty tough were too scared to go to Trenchtown so it meant they knew that I had an idea of what I was talking about and dealing with.

At the end of the first Gunz Down show we did, the kids were going mad and had really loved all the stuff we'd been doing and then the headmaster got up to speak. The kids started to get restless, anticipating the boredom of what he might be about to say to wrap things up, but to their surprise he started telling a story. A few years earlier he'd been running a youth group where a lad, Nathan, had turned up one evening with a knife. Nathan got it out to show his mate Daniel, who jokingly held it up to Nathan's throat. Completely unaware of this, a third lad pushed into the back of Daniel by accident. There was no warning and no time to get the knife out of the way; it went straight through Nathan's main vein and just moments later he died in that teacher's arms. The previously boisterous hall was deathly quiet as the reality of that story sank in. You could have heard a pin drop as they realised what a stupid mistake Nathan had made in bringing the knife, and how his mate had wanted to look hard whereas, instead, another young life was wasted.

A few weeks later at another school a 15-year-old boy, Rakeem, came up to us at the end of the show wearing a bulletproof vest. At first we thought he was messing about but we realised his fear was genuine when we heard that his cousin had been shot, his brother was lying in hospital and he'd been told a gang wanted to kill him. The Gunz Down show gave him an opportunity to be honest with us about how bad things had become in his life and how much serious trouble he'd found himself in. He was on the verge of converting to Islam – like many of the young people attracted by the strong sense of belonging and the passionate call to fight.

Rakeem really affected me and I knew we had to do something to help. The fear haunted me that if we didn't it might not be long before he was dead. I called Les and asked his advice, once again feeling out of my depth. With his own experience of being involved with vicious gangs, Les said he'd be happy to mentor Rakeem, to get involved in his life and see if he could help him find a way out of his current mess. They now meet up regularly and Les even went to the police station when Rakeem was arrested – more than Rakeem's own dad was able to do as he was living in Jamaica.

Recently, as Rakeem was leaving school one afternoon, a member of a rival gang stabbed him in the throat. Charlotte received a phone call from a distraught Natalie (who works in his school) saying she was on her way to see him in the hospital. After they spoke to the doctors we found out the knife was millimetres away from hitting Rakeem's central nerves which would have left him seriously injured. We thanked God he was OK but obviously still have concerns over his safety.

The amazing thing about this incident was that it prompted Natalie to hold a service at her church looking at gang issues. Eight of the kids from school came, deeply affected by seeing Rakeem attacked. There was space in the service for the young people to speak and say how things were from their point of view and one in particular told of how he felt holding a bleeding Rakeem in his arms, not knowing if he would live or die. The church elders prayed for all the young people and five of them gave their lives to Jesus. They still meet up with Natalie and Charlotte to learn more about being a disciple of Jesus.

Giving an opportunity for the young people to talk as well as to listen at the Gunz Down show has been really important, so we also offer to follow up the hour-long assembly with a series of workshops looking at anger management, how to handle conflict, respect and responsibility. This is done in class groups so that they can talk about the issues that impact their decisions regarding guns and knives, such as peer pressure and family environment, in more detail.

As part of the lesson we ask kids what they do when they are angry and a few times people have said that they physically hurt themselves. I was surprised at first, but have realised that self-harm is an increasingly common way for young people to take out the anger and pain they are struggling to express in another, more healthy way. The amazing thing was that because they were able to be so honest, we managed to get them some proper help to deal with this, and our lessons help explore good ways of coping with negative emotions.

The aim of the Gunz Down programme is to achieve real transformation of hearts and minds concerning issues of violence, crime and weapons. Our hope is that by exposing the dark reality of making bad choices, we can inform the young people that there are good life choices to be made and that it's worth being courageous. We know it's hard for them to stand up against their friends and peers but we intend to empower them to choose and give them access to materials that will help them and inspire them to assess their potential actions. We've seen time and time again that wrong choices lead to more wrong choices which eventually lead to people being defined by those choices – choose violence and murder and you will be defined as a violent murderer. What we want to help people to see is that right choices allow them a freedom to choose their own path through life, to explore opportunities and relationships, and to aspire to be like their heroes.

We have been asked to take this to other areas around the country, and while gun crime continues to be a problem we'd love to keep taking Gunz Down to any affected place. We're also aware that there are other issues teenagers in Britain are facing for which they are desperately in need of some advice and help. The statistics and conversations we have with young people about sex and sexual health are incredibly frightening. Over a third of people under the age of 16 have had sex or are in a sexual relationship. In the UK we have one of the highest teenage pregnancy rates in Europe with over a third of pregnancies ending in abortion.

Most of the young people we talk to do not associate sex with love, and we hear the same old stories of young girls being told by their boyfriends, 'If you loved me you would sleep with me.' It's so hard to try and explain to them that they need to protect their hearts as well as their bodies. Much the same as other issues, under-age sex and sleeping around stem from lack of self-esteem, as does the desire to have a baby even without the security of a loving relationship to bring it into. It's now thought that one in ten young people carries the sexually transmitted disease, chlamydia. Although it can be easily treated with antibiotics it often isn't picked up before it is passed on to other sexual partners as it doesn't present many (or sometimes any) symptoms. Left untreated it can lead to infertility. The kids are always shocked when you tell them this. The truth is that teenagers don't want to talk to their parents or their teachers about this stuff and so when we meet them we have the opportunity to be both a listening ear and someone who can give them advice.

We've come to realise that we need the kids to know they can talk to us about anything. It's easy to be shocked when you speak to a 19-year-old who claims to have had over 30 partners or when teenagers tell you they go to 'feel up flats' at lunchtimes just for something to do, but we have to be unshockable. In the church we've had too many taboo subjects which means we don't address them; it's too dangerous to do that with these issues. If we don't talk to the kids about how to make wise decisions they will keep having sex before they are ready. If we don't tell them about STDs and sexual health they will continue sleeping around and spreading diseases. We've found that just by sharing the facts, whole classes have said they'd like to take a chlamydia test which is a fantastic step towards responsible sexual behaviour.

It may have been that when many of us were at school the question was 'Are you going to have sex?' but now it's 'When are you going to have sex?' It's heartbreaking to see so many young people giving themselves so freely, unaware of the implications of what they're doing for both their hearts and their bodies. But it's no good us pointing the finger or tutting over the statistics. We have started running a series of three lessons that cover respect, responsibility and STDs. We've been applying for funding to give us greater opportunities to go into schools and onto estates to deal with this growing issue and are currently writing a show which deals with sexual health.

The hardest thing for me about XLP isn't the struggle for finance and rescources but the feeling of being overwhelmed by the needs there are around us. Seeing Rakeem doing so well and then get stabbed was really hard, and there are often times when a girl will respond really well in lessons on making wise choices and then we'll see her a few months later and she's pregnant. It can be disheartening and you feel like it's an uphill struggle, but the more we see, the more we know we need to be in there helping in whatever way we can. People like Lorna in Trentchtown inspire me to keep going.

14

Conspiracy of the Insignificant

Work with children for any length of time and you'll end up with an amazing amount of stories – the hilarious, the inspirational and the ones that hit you right in the gut. Whenever I do a lesson I like to take some time at the end to do a 'Grill a Christian' session, giving the kids a chance to ask absolutely anything they want to. We've had loads of interesting questions chucked at us including 'Is God white?', 'Who made God?', 'Do you believe in the mark of the beast?' and 'What do you think about the Holocaust?'

One of my favourites was from a little Year 7 boy who, with one minute left to the end of the lesson, said 'What's the point of life?' Anyone got a 60-second answer to that?! At one school in Lewisham a lad called David raised his hand to ask a question. 'If your God is so great,' he said, 'why did he allow this to happen?' He pushed up his blond fringe, showing a nasty scar across his forehead. It was an earnest question but I knew I needed to chat to him outside the lesson to find out more about what was going on.

I invited him to that day's lunch club to talk a bit more and was relieved to see him arrive. He brought a friend with him, Steven, and they told me their stories. David's mum and dad had divorced, his mum drank heavily and got violent with him, one night smashing him over the head with a bottle, leaving him with his scar. David and Steven had both been in and out of foster care and were understandably struggling to get their heads around the idea that there could be a loving God who would allow them to go through so much.

I didn't know what to say; I was at a complete loss. They should never have seen the things they had and I didn't know how to explain an issue to them that many Christians continue to struggle to understand. Although they respected me for not giving them pat answers, it didn't feel like I was doing anything to help.

Then a couple of other kids from their class came over and sat down with us. One of them, Emmanuel, started telling David about his own life, how he too had seen his parents split up and had been abused. He went on to say that he realised that God was with him in the pain and struggles he'd been through. He encouraged David not to blame God, not to get angry and bitter but to find hope in God and a way forward.

I was gobsmacked. If I'd have had a go at answering David's questions it would have been easy to come back to the Fall and Satan but Emmanuel had given a much more articulate and powerful answer as he had related to David out of his own pain. They started to talk and debate God's existence and character and I just sat there in silence, taking it all in, amazed at the very real presence of God in that classroom.

Some of the kids we've met would try anyone's patience. While some are just sweet and lovely, others make you want to tear your hair out with frustration. One person that really springs to mind was Stacey, a 13-year-old girl who had the worst attitude. She was loud, obnoxious, would shout and swear to get attention or to get her own way and would throw things around the room if she was in a bad mood. Stacey came to our lunch club every single week but I can't say it was always good to see her. She was well-known by the pupils, teachers and the XLP team as being a troublemaker and most people would avoid her where possible.

It's embarrassing to admit but it took me a long time before I asked God to give me a better attitude towards Stacey as I was just annoyed at her presence, not wanting to spend more time with her. When I spoke to one of her teachers, they said Stacey came from a complicated family background and Stacey told me herself she would steal neat vodka from her mum's drinks cabinet to block out what was going on at home. Meeting Stacey really made me face up to my bad attitude and reminded me that it's easy to love the lovable but Jesus asks us to love the unlovable too.

As I prayed for Stacey, my heart changed for her. I began to really care about her and we'd often spend time chatting at the lunch clubs or whenever we bumped into each other. One day I saw a New Testament in her pocket and asked her about it. She got a bit embarrassed and didn't want anyone to overhear our conversation but admitted she liked to read it now and then. Once I'd seen it she stopped trying to hide it, and when we had the radio on in a lunch club she tuned it to the Christian station, Premier, and said that she often sneaked into the back of church to listen to the music. It was fantastic to see her developing her own relationship with God and her behaviour changing as a result. Sadly the last time I saw Stacey she was 16 and pregnant. She gave me a big hug and though she seemed happy I was gutted that I hadn't been able to do more to help her.

Sometimes the teachers would ask us to work with specific kids who were having problems in different areas. With Jason it was that he had a hard time controlling his temper and was always getting into fights. Jason was an easy target as he didn't have a proper school uniform and cut his own hair (badly) so other kids were always trying to wind him up, knowing he would rise to it in a flash. I asked Jason to describe the experience of coming to the lunch clubs from his point of view:

I was always in trouble at school, always in fights. It wasn't about winning fights – I rarely started them – but about surviving and getting through another day. My mum kicked me out when I was five and so I went to live with my dad and my stepmother. I don't see my mum; I don't even know where she is as she never contacts me.

My friends and I started going to the XLP lunch club, Extreme, and I enjoyed playing the games and having a laugh with my mates. After a while I started listening more to the things Patrick and the team were saying about God, and they started to make more sense to me. I made friends with the XLP team and thought they were all really cool and were always interested in me and what was going on in my life.

When they started doing an after-school club I went along and that was where I gave my life to God. As I prayed I felt my spine begin to tingle and ever since my heart's been on fire for God. Even in the winter I don't feel the cold and people are always asking why I don't wear a coat even when it's snowing. It's God's Spirit that keeps me warm now.

Before I started doing the XLP lunch club I was on the verge of being kicked out of school for always having fights, but the more I got to know about God, the less I seemed to get in trouble. Going to the lunch club gave me something to belong to and it boosted my self-confidence. I didn't have many friends before so it really meant something to me to have somewhere to be, and I couldn't believe it when I realised Jesus was not only my Saviour but also the best friend I could ever have.

My teachers can't believe how much I've improved and I even got one of the highest marks in our end-of-term tests which would never have happened before.

I've stayed out of trouble for a while now. People still try and wind me up because I used to be an easy target but now I just calm myself down and while I don't let them walk all over me, I don't use my fists anymore. My bedroom has marks in the wall where I would punch it when I was really angry – when I see them it just reminds me how far I've come.

I've started playing guitar and writing songs to God because I just want to worship him and tell people what he's done for me. Recently I gave my testimony at church and one of my mates came along and when he heard it he became a Christian too – it was the best feeling. When I leave school I'd love to do the XLP year-out eXperience and then maybe go on to be a youth worker so I can help other people who feel as isolated as I did, because what XLP have done for me has completely changed my life.

Last time I saw Jason at school he'd got hold of a flyer for a Soul in the City event we were doing and had printed loads out. Off his own bat he'd laminated them and was giving them out to other young people in the school. It was fantastic to see him just wanting to tell others about the joy he'd found in God. We got a real boost seeing the initiative he'd shown in advertising the event; it showed just how far he'd come from when we first met him.

As you will have seen from many of the stories I have told you, working in schools and in inner-city areas isn't really about big and spectacular events. No one may ever see that you helped one young person to read, but the time spent with them, building their skills and their confidence, may help them get an education which will vastly improve their prospects in life. Add to that what it communicates – that someone cared enough to take time out of their day-to-day life to be there for them – and that will speak volumes to the young person and reassure them that someone cares.

Since we value working with the kids in this way, it can be hard to quantify what we do. It's not about having a high 'conversion rate' – while we love to talk about our faith and it is the reason we do everything we do, we know that God wants us to work with these young people and help them whether they choose to believe in him or not. We don't know what happens to most of the kids we work with and rarely do we know the long-term impact we've had on them.

It could be that the team gives someone the confidence to go for their dream and they go on to do something huge with their life, like find a cure for a deadly disease. It may be that having confidence makes them realise they have options in life other than to deal drugs. Maybe through a lesson you stop someone from making a bad decision about when they choose to have sex, another from getting a gun and ending up dead from a turf war. While of course we'd love to know, we have to commit each person to God and his ultimate care and know that we can only play our part, but to remember that he does call us to play a part.

In many ways it's not about seeing what some would consider as spectacular results, as what we'd love to see is those who have been written off by society going on to lead 'normal' lives, i.e. not going to prison, not getting pregnant in their teenage years and not dying young because they got mixed up in violent gangs. We want the young people to be able to gain qualifications and get a job rather than resort to crime because they think they have no options.

Sometimes it feels to us, as we're doing these small acts, as though we're just chucking out mustard seeds. We don't always see how they grow or even get appreciation for playing our part but when we come before God we do have the reassurance that we're growing his kingdom. When Jesus talked about mustard seeds he said they were the smallest of the seeds but they become the largest of the garden plants.[1]

Like many people I've been completely inspired by hearing about the words and works of Mother Teresa. One of the things I love about her story is that at school the best thing they found to say about her on her yearly report was that she was good at putting out candles! Can you believe that the woman who went on to be one of the best-known missionaries the world has ever seen, had so little going for her? She went on to feed 500,000 hungry people every year, helped those with leprosy, and gave dignity and comfort to those who were dying in the streets. It clearly wasn't obvious to her teachers that she was destined to be famous the world over

---

[1] Matthew 13:32

and become an icon of self-sacrificing service with her own place in the history books.

The thing that made all the difference to Mother Teresa was her love for Jesus, and the secret to her years of tireless service seems to be that she was never condescending in what she did. She saw Jesus in the eyes of the poor and so she faithfully served them with the love she would have shown if it had been the Lord right in front of her. When the kids are driving us mad at school, not listening and being annoying, or when money is tight and we don't know how we'll continue, it really helps to remember that what we're doing is about worship. Every young person we try and help, every small seed we sow, is us showing our love to God. As Mother Teresa said,

> I don't want the work to become a business but to remain a work of love. Take him at his word and seek first the kingdom of God and all else will be added on. Joy, peace and unity are more important than money.

If our motivation is to grow a big ministry or to get a name for ourselves, we'll soon run out of steam, but if we take Mother Teresa's example and do everything out of our love for God and a compassion for those around us, we can trust that he will give us all we need to keep going. There's no quick-fix solution; if we want to see change, we have to be in it for the long haul.

We now run 60 lunch clubs every month, help over 20 young people read, see over 200 young people come to the bus each week, run four art showcases which bring us in touch with 150 young people, run three large London-wide tours a year, and take hundreds of lessons on every subject you can imagine. We help over 15 churches with their youth work through our gap-year course, have a school in Ghana and continue to undertake a number of mission trips each year. We're expanding into other London boroughs and have been learning a lot through working in one that is predominantly Muslim.

We'd really like to learn more and develop our connections with both the Muslim and Asian communities. One of our team, Tom, has been working with excluded kids in one borough, filming TV programmes about the issues they are facing. The films have then been shown in all the different classes in that school and have provoked interesting discussion and debate.

As more people have heard of what we're doing, we have been approached by churches, councils, MPs and the police who'd like us to work in their area. Sometimes it's tempting just to focus on South East London where we've been working for years, but we've felt God has challenged us to keep giving away all that he has given us. We don't want to bite off more than we can chew but we've suggested to other boroughs and cities in the country that if they employ someone who we can help to train and mentor, we'll help in any way that we can and let them use the XLP brand so they can go into schools and do similar stuff to what we do.

There's no special formula to what we've done and it could be replicated (and no doubt bettered!) in any town, city or village across the country and the world. Only God can change people's hearts, but we can listen, be approachable and lend a helping hand where needed. God longs to use all of us to bring glory to himself if we will just make ourselves available and not be so busy we miss what he's saying to us. You have to remember, too, that because you may come from a background which is different from those you are trying to reach, it doesn't mean you can't reach them, but it's about stepping into their world and understanding where they are coming from. We know we're not 'it' and we don't have all the answers; we're on a journey where we're trying to hear God . . . and I encourage you to keep doing the same. I promise you, if God can use the likes of me and the XLP team then he can use you!

When I think about how XLP came about and the things God has done through it, I can best sum it up by borrowing some of Paul's words to the Ephesians:

> When it came to presenting the Message to people who had no background in God's way, I was the least qualified of any of the available Christians. God saw to it that I was equipped, but you can be sure it had nothing to do with my natural abilities. And so here I am, preaching and writing about things that are way over my head, the inexhaustible riches and generosity of Christ.[2]

One of my favourite quotes is from General Booth's last speech to the Salvation Army, in which he gave a sort of summary of what drove him on in his lifetime:

> While women weep, as they do now, I'll fight. While little children go hungry, as they do now, I'll fight. While men go to prison, in and out, in and out, as they do now, I'll fight. While there is a drunkard left, while there is a poor lost girl upon the streets, while there remains one dark soul without the light of God, I'll fight – I'll fight to the very end!

And he did. Why shouldn't we?

---

[2] Ephesians 3, *The Message*

Get in Touch with XLP

If you'd like to get in touch with Patrick, find out more about working in schools, or would be interested in applying for the eXperience Gap Year programme (which starts in September each year), please email info@xlp.org.uk

On our website (www.xlp.org.uk) you can find out more about XLP, how you can support our work, read our latest news and sign up for our newsletter.

For more information on Gunz Down please see www.gunzdown.com

For more information on Ghana please visit www.aaco.org.uk